FOREV

RAVISHING
Love

Devotions on Encountering
God in the Heavenly Realm

NANCY ANN JOHNSON

Ravishing Love

Text and Cover Design: Carol Martinez

ISBN: 979-8-9897130-0-4

engagingjesus.com

TABLE OF CONTENTS

TABLE OF CONTENTS

FOREWORD

A church experienced a visitation of the Holy Spirit and power in the late 1980s. During an evening when the leadership had gathered for a holiday celebration, the Holy Spirit fell on all in attendance. None had encountered the power of the Lord previously, and they did not even believe the gifts of the Spirit were relevant for today. Yet, that night, many shook and trembled under his power and spontaneously began to prophesy. This went on for days and weeks following, and more and more of the church members experienced similar encounters. Before long, the church assembly looked very different than it had previously.

In the presence of the Lord, the entire church was transformed. When I visited the church almost a decade later, there was no trace of the previous conservative personality of the congregation. The church was full of fiery faith and passion, prophetic flow, and power. You could tell that many in this body of believers who carried great anointings had "been with Jesus."

Transformation takes place in his presence— not at a school desk or through an intense seminary program. Even though biblical knowledge and training are helpful and commendable, on their own they will not transform. We are to be people of presence and as a result, ultimately people of power and encounter.

I love the story in Acts 4:13 where Peter and John were moving in supernatural power and people were in awe. Look at what the Bible says regarding them:

> "Now as they observed the confidence of Peter and John and understood that they were uneducated and untrained men, they were amazed, and **began to recognize them as having been with Jesus.**"

They knew they were uneducated and untrained, and yet they carried such presence and power. How could this be? **—Because, they had been with Jesus!**

Presence transforms! Relationship with God connects you to his heart. Nancy Johnson is truly a woman who engages in divine presence and profound relationship. She seeks the Lord regularly and experiences realms of his glory. She is passionate to see others engaged in his glory and to know his love. I have seen her mentor and nurture many into glory encounters.

Ravishing Love is a daily devotional containing short meditations and scripture verses that call you to explore the unconditional adoration that he has lavished upon you. As you meditate on the scriptures and the insights given, I am confident that you will feel the call to explore his heart and his love in deeper ways than you have known previously. When you are full due to basking in his presence and receiving divine revelations, you are then ready to go and pour out his love on others. The fragrance of that love will attract many to him.

When you leave his presence, don't be surprised if people say to you, "I recognize that you have been with Jesus." That is the goal of this devotional.

Thank you, Nancy Johnson, for paying the price in his presence so we may partake of the treasures found in this lovely devotional. Well done.

Patricia King,

Founder, Patricia King Ministries

INTRODUCTION

This book is about being captivated by the one who burns day and night for us. His name is Jesus. He is a man of passion—fire from the waist up and fire from the waist down. He wants us fastened to his heart and lavished by his love. His affection is unmatched by anything on this earth. And the joy of being loved by him will thrill your life. He is supernaturally far above all we can imagine, dream, or think, yet he invites us to know him intimately. His heart is that you be kissed awake to abide in his love forever. He is precious beyond measure, and you will find him in these words and all the spaces in between. The new era is all about becoming one with our magnificent King.

He calls you as his child to come up to his heavenly throne in glory with him, where he can show you things to come. He wants you to get to know him, not only through studying the Bible, but by encountering the real living Word, Jesus himself. The world has tried everything to keep people from recognizing God. But he is alive and tangible. The Bible says: "This is eternal life, to know him." So, it's time to build a relationship with him. Jesus profoundly expressed his heart when he told the people of the time that even if they prophesied or drove out demons, they would not be able to say he was Lord without intimacy with him. He would tell them plainly: "I never knew you." The point is he wants an intimate and passionate relationship with us.

As a young child, I went to church with my parents. But I never really met Jesus as a true and living friend who would walk with me until I almost died. Giving my life to Jesus at that time and being born again changed my life forever. He miraculously healed me and set me back on my feet to live again. Pain and hopelessness had been part of my daily life as I struggled with an incurable illness. Yet, as a newly saved and healed believer, I entered into the meaning of life and the discovery that my Creator is LOVE and he is bursting with good news and good plans for me. Since then, I have been in pursuit of this magnificent King who saved my life. He is the one thing, the only thing that will satisfy the heart that is longing for love and restoration. I found him in the Scriptures, with the body of Christ, on the streets with the lost, in family, in worship, in nature, and so much more. Sharing his love is everything to me, and serving him is the joy of my life.

These devotions were written by waiting on the Lord and listening intently to him with every one of my senses.

Then I was able to explain what he wanted to say, going deeper into his mysteries and personality. I have practiced the Presence of God and led prophetic prayer meetings for years. I learned it is about engaging him heart-to-heart in union and connecting deeply with him in dialog. I started by setting up a chair for Jesus during my prayer time. Then, as my spirit grew and I became hungrier, I also added a chair for the Father and the Holy Spirit. I came to know each of them individually as I journaled, and they led me through my Bible. What a joy it was getting to know God as he came and encountered me. It's a daily adventure for sure! I fell in love with journaling as I listened for and heard the voice of God.

It has been a pleasure to write these devotions with the Lord. I pray that his heart and mind be felt tangibly on the following pages and that you will encounter him profoundly. His presence and wisdom overflow the pages, especially regarding the revelation of your identity and sonship. You are his child, meant to run your race in his arms forever, falling ever deeper in love with him. Use this book to develop intimacy with the Lord and learn your identity and how he sees and knows you. You have rights and privileges as a child of God, and he wants you to know about them. You have been raised up with Christ the exalted One, and seated with him in the glorious perfection and authority of the heavenly realm. He wants you to be powerful and has strategically put these devotions together to lead you through encounter into deeper truth.

Heavenly Engagements

At the end of every ten devotions, you will find a heavenly engagement to encounter God. They are all about entering the Kingdom of God as a child. My prayer is that you would be relaxed in the Lord's stillness and meditate deeply as you read slowly, over and over. Let your spirit lead you into all truth as you pray for him to walk you into these heavenly adventures through the scripture. Scripture is alive, and God is waiting enthusiastically to meet with you. It looks like imagination at first, but then you realize that the Holy Spirit has begun to awaken your spirit eyes (the eyes of your imagination. See Ephesians 1:18). Your other spiritual senses will also start to come alive as well. We are used to using all our natural senses. But God wants to awaken our ability to see, taste, touch, hear, and smell by the power of the Holy Spirit. Ask the Holy Spirit to sanctify all the gates of your senses with the blood of Jesus and to guide you into all truth. He will heal you on many levels as you read about and encounter him.

I pray that the living Word, Jesus Christ, captivates your heart forever and encounters you with his limitless love every day of your life. May you be a friend of God who connects with him in a glorious relationship on earth and in heaven. All of creation is groaning for you, as his bride, to walk in the fullness of God. Be delivered and set free by the finished work of the cross. As his child, I pray that you would entangle your heart with his and be lost forever in the divine dance of the Trinity.

Forever in His Heart,
Nancy Johnson

Arise, my darling!
Come quickly, my beloved.
Come and be the graceful gazelle with me.
Come and be like a dancing deer with me.
We will dance in the high place of the sky,
yes, on the mountains of fragrant spice.

Forever we shall be united as one!

Song of Solomon 8:14 TPT

ASCENSION

Through you I ascend to the highest peaks of your glory to stand in the heavenly places, strong and secure in you.

Psalm 18:33 TPT

I wanted to offer you breathtaking wonder! So I gave you myself on that cross. Will you live through me? Inside of Christ? In the bliss of our relationship, you and I can ascend to the highest peaks. I have rescued you and brought you into a beautiful, broad place of light. I live on the dazzling mountain tops of glory. Love me with all your heart and get lost in my magnificence. You are worthy in this place. The atmosphere overflows with love and countless angels. Let me wrap you with affection.

Here you can stand in heavenly places and bask in the sunshine of my love. You now have all the rights as a family member to my household. You are strong and mighty, beloved. You stand secure with the greatest valiant warriors, all heroes of the faith. My cloud of witnesses is cheering for you. You were the joy set before me. Keep looking to me; I will lead you forth into great victory!

Jesus, I ascend to the highest peaks of glory in the heavenly places. For you, my sweet Jesus, are my holy obsession! I gaze upon you on the dazzling mountain tops. My beloved King of Kings and Lord of Lords, receive my surrendered heart.

Psalm 18:19

Ephesians 2:19

Hebrews 12:1-2

COME UP HERE!

*Then suddenly...I saw a heavenly portal open before
me, and the same trumpet-voice I heard speaking
with me at the beginning broke the silence and said,
"Ascend into this realm! I want to reveal to you what
must happen after this."*

Revelation 4:1 TPT

Let the high praises of God resound! And my Spirit
will lift you high! Children enter my courts with
praise and thanksgiving. I am the open door. Cease striving and enter my rest. I want you right here with me in
glory. It all works by simple faith. This realm is not far off
because there is no distance in the Spirit. Your hunger is
the secret key that gets past the busy mind.

I want to reveal myself to you high and lifted up. Ask
me and I will tell you mysteries. Listen for my still,
small voice; I am always speaking to you in so many
ways. Visions, dreams, knowings; be sensitive to them
all. Let us dance in divine romance. Like Abraham
and Moses, you can change the world when you cry
out to me.

Jesus, you are showing me how to ascend into your heavenly courts. I will enter in with childlike faith and pray out your love plan. Thank you that as I hear and see what you are doing, your Kingdom will come on earth as it is in heaven.

Psalm 27:4

Jeremiah 33:3

John 17:24

LIVING FROM ZION

*By contrast, we have already come near to God
in a totally different realm, the Zion-realm, for we
have entered the city of the Living God, which is
the New Jerusalem in heaven! We have joined
the festal gathering of myriads of angels in their
joyous celebration!*

Hebrews 12:22 TPT

Royal sons and daughters, you have come to the glittering city, the Zion realm of God! Ho! My work is complete on the cross. My beauty, you are forgiven! You are here in the Spirit, and I have promised you free access to the bliss of my presence. I am the door! I long to keep your attention here. I know the world tries to lure you away. But you are no longer conformed to this world.

My children have special privileges to be beside me, even seated with me. Come to the wedding banquet! Don't settle for the crumbs under the table, beloved. Be bold.

I have chosen you to rule and reign with me in glory. Bring heaven to earth with your decrees as you dance with the angels of light in joyous celebration.

Jesus, my one desire is to be with you! I open my spiritual eyes and all my senses to the joyous splendor of the New Jerusalem. There is no more separation. I am living my life in the light of Zion, declaring your will, and dancing with the angels in praise.

Ephesians 3:12

Ephesians 2:6

1 Peter 2:9

YOU ARE WORTHY

Yahweh, who dares to dwell with you? Who pre-
sumes the privilege of being close to you, living next
to you in your shining place of glory?

Psalm 15:1 TPT

I proclaim the truth to you, Zion dweller! You have been made worthy by Jesus! It is through him that you can dwell with me in glory. You are seated with me. You are priceless, privileged, and favored. In fact, all the blessings of Abraham have come upon you. Yes, I want you right next to me, at my right hand. You say, "I am not worthy." But I declare that you are a crown of splendor, my bride, and a jewel in my hand. Your heritage is staggering. You are exceedingly beautiful and valuable in Jesus, shining righteousness and salvation to the nations. Be confident in my love for you. I set a guard over you; keeping, protecting, and delighting over you incessantly.

I release to you an insatiable appetite for the beauty of my holiness. You are set apart for me and are made for oneness. It is with great pleasure that I draw you close. Gratefully wrap yourself around me in joyous freedom.

Those who entwine themselves to me will renew their strength, for I am the source of life itself. I explode with energy and glory power—receive it all. It is yours for the asking. Come, I am making you the flame of my desire!

Yes, Lord! I joyfully come up to Zion and dance forever in your glory. I am worthy to be a crown of splendor and a jewel in your hand because of Jesus. Wahoo! I am beautifully wrapped around you as your flame of desire!

Hebrews 12:22-24

Isaiah 62:1-3

Isaiah 40:31

MOUNTAIN OF THE LORD

Many peoples will come and say, "Everyone, come!
Let's go up higher to Yahweh's mountain, to the
house of Jacob's God; then he can teach us his
ways, and we can walk in his paths!" Zion will be
the center of instruction, and the word of Yahweh
will go out from Jerusalem.

Isaiah 2:3 TPT

Come to the heights of my splendid city in heaven! Soar on my wings of love. I desire to see your lovely face and keep you safe. In my house, there are many mansions. You have a place of authority here by me in paradise. It is your supernatural home now, and where I am, you are. You live in a new creation reality and are a citizen of heaven. Celebrate with my angels!

I will draw you with my love. I will teach you my ways of victory as you sit with me. I have many pearls of wisdom to gift to you. Hold onto everything I have taught you. Let your life be a display of integrity, and you will succeed. Rest and snuggle in my light with me right now, and believe I am infusing you with my creative solutions.

Jesus, I live in the high place of Mount Zion every day. I love to sit with you in the royal courts of heaven and receive your wisdom. I live in continual awareness and attentiveness to you. I am blessed to rule and reign from heaven!

Hebrews 12:22

Philippians 3:20

John 14:1-3

ENTHRONED IN PRAISES

Yet I know that you are most holy; it's indisputable.
You are God-Enthroned, surrounded with songs,
living among the shouts of praise of your princely
people.

Psalm 22:3 TPT

My faithfulness to you is legendary! One minute soaring in the anointed atmosphere of heaven will forever capture your heart. Put on the garments of praise for the spirit of heaviness. Be wrapped in light. Let me have your heart as you shout and praise; I will enthrone you with my presence. The government of my peace extends forever. Wahoo! I will scatter your enemies in my supreme sovereignty. The battle is mine.

Everyone praises the beauty of my holiness! Their wild-hearted worship thrills my heart. Even the trees of the fields shall clap their hands. Bring me glory by shouting, dancing, and twirling. I love your expressive thanksgiving! I love it! I live here in this place—pulsing and alive within the symphony of your songs. My kings and queens adore me. Let the joy of praise fill you with a merry heart.

Jesus, my heart explodes with praise and ecstatic worship. I am wrecked by your personal love for me. May my worship ravish your heart. I create an atmosphere of adoration for you continuously!

Isaiah 61:3

Psalm 100:4

Isaiah 55:12

HAMMERS FROM HEAVEN

"Is not my word like a fire?" says the Lord, *"And like a hammer that breaks the rock in pieces?*

Jeremiah 23:29 NKJV

Oh, you can have so much fun when you get a word from heaven. You can stand on it, sow it, expect it, and rejoice over the harvest. The best place to use your hammer is from the throne room. It's so much more potent than from Earth. A king will decree a thing, and it will come to pass. So be seated as my king, priest, and prophet. Do it up here with me in glory. Yes, it will be like a fire that breaks through rocks.

If I put a word in your heart, and you proclaim it, it works like a hammer. It works just like explosive lightning coming out of your mouth. It is a supernatural phenomenon. Yes, my word will go forth and accomplish what I have purposed for it. It is my holy word and my promise. It brings health to your body and strength to your bones. Sow it with confidence, and you will reap a harvest. Keep your heart tender before me as you wait on my timing. Keep hammering with faith, and the rocks will break to pieces. Be sure to make ample use of your imagination, too. See it happening in the Spirit. Get ready! I am releasing the hammers from heaven.

Jesus, thank you that you are giving me a new power-filled hammer from heaven. I will come and hear what you are saying and release it with joy from your heart in heaven. It will easily break through every rock of resistance and make way for your good plan on the Earth.

Isaiah 55:11

Proverbs 3:8

Job 22:28

FILL YOUR THOUGHTS
WITH HEAVEN

Christ's resurrection is your resurrection too. This is why we are to yearn for all that is above, for that's where Christ sits enthroned at the place of all power, honor, and authority! Yes, feast on all the treasures of the heavenly realm and fill your thoughts with heavenly realities, and not with the distractions of the natural realm.

Colossians 3:1-2 TPT

I AM seated at the brilliant center of power over the universe. And this is your royal light-filled home too. I have resurrected you and established you. Let your every thought be captivated by my love. You are seated here with me in the Spirit. Authority, power, and honor are yours.

Let childlike curiosity rule your heart. Ask me questions. I am eager to show you around! Be fascinated with my face; let all your senses be open. Keep focused and catch the little foxes that try to distract. My throne is sapphire.

It has rainbows, streets of gold, angels, seven Spirits burning, creatures, 24 elders, and much more. Feast on all of the riches of my wisdom and knowledge. Just close your eyes, and as you meditate on me with desire, it's all here for you.

Jesus, I feast on all the treasures of your heavenly realities. Show me your glory, Lord! I ask for a pure heart so that I would see God. I gladly exchange this world for yours. I live the Christ life now!

Ephesians 2:4-8

Isaiah 6:1-7

Revelation 4:1-11

_____

_____

_____

BEHOLD MY GLORY

In the year that King Uzziah died, I clearly saw the Lord. He was seated on his exalted throne, towering high above me. His long, flowing robe of splendor spread throughout the temple.

Isaiah 6:1 TPT

Children, come and gaze upon my royal beauty, and you will be transformed into the same image from glory to glory. The sacrifice has been made, and the veil has been torn. You have free access, little one. My robe of splendor fills the temple in gorgeous heavenly colors. Wrap yourself in its wonder, flowing with endless holiness. I offer you paradise, my darling.

There is a place of ascension in worship where I enthrone you in your praises. I surround you, cover you, and pour out my Spirit of wisdom and revelation, enlightening your eyes. You are made to seek my face and to behold my glory. Be with me where I am—for I love us to be together. I am accelerating the seer anointing all over the world. Abide in me, come and sit with me. You will become a mirror reflecting my glory. Will you come away with me?

Jesus, I am blessed to have eyes that gaze upon you in your royal splendor. I gratefully let go of the world to have you as my beloved. Every day, my eyes are gaining more and more clarity. I receive the seer anointing with great joy!

Matthew 27:51

Ephesians 1:17-18

2 Corinthians 3:18

MY DOOR IS OPEN

Yahweh, I love to live in your house, this dwelling place of dazzling glory!

Psalm 26:8 TPT

Oh yes! Come to explore with the Holy Spirit! My home is your home. Explore all the rooms, chambers, and hallways. Fling wide all the doors. Inside each door are new dimensions and more layers of my goodness. Play to your heart's desire. Receive everything I have for you. You even have permission to dwell in my house. A Father's house is open to his children. My child, you are a very special member of my household.

The atmosphere of my home is full of sparkling glory light. Bask in the sunshine of my loving Spirit. The beauty of holiness is on full display as heavenly music washes over every level. Wisdom rejoices endlessly. Let us praise! Splash in my crystal clear, living waters! They will fill you with joyous laughter. Will you come?

I declare you will dwell in the secret place with me, for I treasure our intimate times together.

Father, I will come to dwell in your house. I will explore it all—every room, hallway, and chamber is just for me! I am so excited to accept your invitation. Yes, I am intimately yours!

Ephesians 2:19

Revelations 22:1

Psalm 91:1

HEAVENLY ADVENTURES

Engagement

Imagine that in the King's house there are many mansions. As you walk up a beautiful stairway, you will see a door. It is gorgeous and alive and vibrant and glowing with glory. And Jesus is inviting you to walk through that door. Throw it open wide. On the other side, you will see beautiful glory, rainbows, and waterfalls. He is asking you to come away with him. As you enter the door, Jesus takes your hand and walks you proudly down a beautiful path. You look into his eyes and see his love sparkling at you. Coming to a promenade of pillars down a golden street, you see up ahead seven torches blazing in stunning beauty. Be in awe of his splendor. You come upon another door, and Jesus says, "This is my home." He says, "I am flinging wide open all the doors of my house to you. You can run through the halls and the doors. It's your time to play like a curious child that enters right in. Let your imagination discover everything." As you walk with him, be curious and ask: "Jesus, show me the rainbows. Jesus, show me your throne. Jesus, show me your storage rooms." Let your desire be that he takes you on a tour.

Have the most joyous time celebrating because you have complete access. His home is open to you. Bask in the sunshine of his face. Wrap your arms around him, and he will hold and love you endlessly. Worship and dance with him forever. Ask him what scripture promise he has for you today. Ask him if there is anything you need to know. You are a dearly loved and cherished member of the family.

_____

_____

_____

MY FATHER'S PASSION

And as Jesus rose up out of the water, the heavenly
realm opened up over him and he saw the Holy
Spirit descend out of the heavens and rest upon him
in the form of a dove. Then suddenly the voice of the
Father shouted from the sky, saying, "This is the Son
I love, and my greatest delight is in him."

Matthew 3:16-17 TPT

My dearest one, our Father is shouting with his thundering voice over you! He is splitting open the heavens for you on every side, giving you every advantage, including sending the Holy Spirit to rest upon you too. Receive this beautiful gift as his magnificent child. Your life now in Christ is a journey into his heart. Get ready for him to show you great and mighty things—his mysteries and treasures. He absolutely delights in you.

You will grow in stature and favor with God and men like me. He will reward, establish, and affirm you. You must hear his proud voice shouting, my child. His love will thrill your heart to no end. He loves to bless and to be generous to you. Let him express all his love languages.

He loves you just as he loves me. We are one! You and I are one, and the Father loves us in our togetherness.

Jesus, thank you for expressing Father's passionate love. Shout and sing over me, Father! You have a big heart of love for me, too, and I will run into your arms. I am safe in your secret place of thunder. I receive your precious Holy Spirit to rest upon me. Touch me with your tenderness and compassion, and send my heart soaring on the highest winds of joy. Father, I am yours!

John 17:23

Isaiah 42:1

Luke 2:52

KEY TO AWARENESS

I have set the Lord always before me; Because He is
at my right hand I shall not be moved.

Psalm 16:8 NKJV

Pursue me with passion and holy flames of desire. King David was a man after my heart. He was a God-chaser on every level. Like David, set me always before you. Never take your gaze off me because this is an adventure that requires face-to-face. I know your mind wanders, but say no to thinking, and drink in my presence instead. You can keep your focus steady by learning to follow my thoughts and what pleases me. I love renewing your mind with my Word and prayer and worship.

When my children come to earth, many lose touch with me in their hearts. The world has a way of luring them away. But there is no good thing I will withhold from you. You can have as much of my goodness as you desire. Every time you engage me, imagine me before you. Become aware of me in the stillness. Cease striving and breathe deeply of my loving peace. I will guide you steadily through the twists and turns of life. Keep me at your right hand, and the world will not move you.

I want you to be conscious of me on every level, using every one of your senses. Taste my goodness. I am living and I am right here with you! I am continually blessing you in little whispers and nudges. You may not necessarily see me, but by faith, you may have a knowing or a recurring thought that's from me. I will never leave you nor forsake you!

Jesus, I decree I will pursue you with a holy passion. My eyes continually gaze upon you. My confidence will never be shaken because you are right beside me and within me. Mighty God, I trust that you are always with me.

Hebrews 11:27

Hebrews 12:1-2

Ephesians 1:18

HIS ROSE

I am truly his rose, the very theme of his song. I'm overshadowed by his love, growing in the valley!

Song of Solomon 2:1 TPT

There is much to sing about you! You have chosen me, and it ravishes my heart. I clutch you to my heart throughout your life in constant song. Oh, what beauty! Oh, what fragrance! Oh, what bliss! When you choose to love me, your heart will open like a rose and release a wondrous perfume. Like a tiny drop in a pond, it will affect everything.

My beautiful heavenly rose! You delight me in every way. Just one glance from your eyes of love and my heart is ravished. You are fresh and new every morning, ready to shine my light everywhere. I love to come to your garden and gaze through the lattice. There is no one like you in the whole world. You glisten with love as I surround you on every side, covering and overshadowing you. Rest in my love and care. I care for you jealously.

Jesus, I am astonished by your unconditional love. I was unquestionably dark, yet you forgave it all. I want to know more about how much you love me! Yes, I adore being your rose. I fling my heart wide open to you!

Song of Solomon 4:9

Song of Solomon 4:10

Song of Solomon 2:9

OUTSTANDING AMONG TEN THOUSAND

He alone is my beloved. He shines in dazzling splendor yet is still so approachable—without equal as he stands above all others, outstanding among ten thousand!

Song of Solomon 5:10 TPT

Just as I am your bridegroom, pre-eminent among ten thousand, I see you as matchless in beauty. There is no one like you. Stunning, innocent, and without guile. Yes, I am without equal, but my door is constantly flung wide open to everyone who hungers. My heart is gentle and lowly and you are welcome. Even though it may seem like you are a million miles away from perfection, I look at you through the sanctifying blood of Christ. Rejoice with the angels! Above all others, I alone am your God!

I see you standing before my courts of glory. Your soul hungering, longing to catch a glimpse of the beauty of my holiness. I'll tell you a secret. Your passionate worship ravishes my heart, taking my breath away. If you take one step towards me, I will take 1,000 towards you. Get ready. I will not tame my love! I will pursue you to the depths and thrill your heart with ecstatic bliss. Together our hearts will explode in unison!

Lord, I decree that my heart will have all of your fiery love! Wow! Passion and hunger ignite my entire being. You alone are my desire and my chief among ten thousand.

Psalm 42:1

Song of Solomon 6:5

Zephaniah 3:17

_____

_____

_____

HIGHWAY OF LIGHT

But the lovers of God walk on the highway of light,
and their way shines brighter and brighter
until they bring forth the perfect day.

Proverbs 4:18 TPT

You are on my love path! Glorious light and life embellish this highway. It is like the light of dawn in its glistening, quiet beauty. I have kissed you with my breath of life. We are together now, united as one. Rejoice in our righteous path, a lifestyle of holiness and wholehearted devotion. This is the ever-spiraling light of our DNA in divine entanglement. We dance, we sing, and we create a dazzling mystery.

My ways are pure. My ways are holy. My ways are just. You will shine brighter and brighter, my friend. You are going from glory to glory, for I will teach and bring you forth. Just as there is no hurry to create the finest art, your perfection is worth the wait, for you are my workmanship and my heritage. Look into my eyes—I have said it and will do it. I am creating in you the full stature of Christ and the perfect day.

Wow, Father, I run to follow you fully until you bring me forth perfectly! I am blessed with your ever-spiraling DNA now. I love to please you with all my heart. Make me humble and teachable so I can walk in your ways of holiness.

Ephesians 2:10

Psalm 119:73

Numbers 23:19

49

FATHERED BY GOD

Those who are loved by God, let his love continually
pour from you to one another, because God is love.
Everyone who loves is fathered by God and experi-
ences an intimate knowledge of him. The one who
doesn't love has yet to know God, for God is love.

1 John 4:7-8 TPT

Beautiful children who have yet to know me, enter my courts of love. I am a dance of love, an embrace of love, a song of love. I am the creator of love. Come, come, come. Climb on my lap; you will find me gentle, humble, and kind. I am a Father who adores holding, comforting, healing, and playing with my family. Rejoice! Live in the fullness of life, be well-loved, and give it generously away to others.

I want you drenched with liquid love. I will never contain it, nor should you. My love pours into the darkness and brings it back to life. Set my passion loose through you, and all will bloom into its original beauty. From the beginning to the end, this is my love language. My children, hear my heart; I yearn for our oneness! I am not satisfied without you!

Father, yes, yes, yes! I am thrilled to be your child! I love you with all my heart, mind, soul, and might. I want to overflow with your unconditional sweet love. Father me, Lord, and help me become your love to others.

1 John 3:1

Ephesians 2:4-10

1 John 4:16

RAVISHING LOVE

*Rivers of pain and persecution will never extinguish
this flame. Endless floods will be unable to quench
this raging fire that burns within you. Everything will
be consumed. It will stop at nothing as you yield
everything to this furious fire until it won't even
seem to you like a sacrifice anymore.*

Song of Solomon 8:7 TPT

Beloved, I have placed a flame within you that burns
to love me. This jealous, all-consuming love burns
hot with desire. It devours all. It is about one thing; having more of me! Nothing can stop it, and no flood can
douse it. It will burn out every thought, every stronghold, every deception, and every distraction.

Forget about problems. They are nothing before my ravishing love. Dance with the one who died to give you
everything. I will thrill your entire being with first love
and power. Look into my eyes, my bride. I love to be
loved! Our adoration lights up the whole universe in a
gorgeous display of color!

Lay down every pain—trade in trials and tribulations for more of me. Center yourself in my glorious flame. I want nothing more than to form your precious heart into pure gold.

Jesus, burn in me! Nothing will extinguish my passionate love for you! I want the breadth, the length, the height, and the depth of your love to consume everything in me. Make me the flame of your desire!

1 Peter 1:5-9

1 John 4:16

Ephesians 3:16-20

OVERSHADOWED

*While he was still speaking, a bright cloud overshad-
owed them, and behold, a voice out of the cloud
said, "This is My beloved Son, with whom I am well-
pleased; listen to Him!"*

Matthew 17:5 NASB

My children, I am showing up in clouds of glory
worldwide. I am not limited to meetings. I am
breaking out and going viral. My voice shouts from the
cloud: "I have no walls and no limits." Listen carefully
and follow the cloud. I am going mobile; the wheels of
my Spirit go straight ahead, and they don't turn to the
right or the left. They follow where the Spirit leads. See,
I am doing a new thing!

I will overshadow you just like Mary. She joyfully
cried out, "I am your handmaiden, Lord! Let it be to
me according to your word." Rest under my shadow,
beloved. I am just getting started blessing you to be fruitful, to take dominion, and to multiply.

Let me show you grand visions like Ezekiel. I want my
presence to be so captivating in your life that people are

overwhelmed by my glory everywhere you go. Listen, you have full access to me because the veil is already torn. I am more than willing to show you the heavenly realms. Let us run together into my cloud filled chamber.

Oh, Father, overshadow me! Captivate me! I want your bright cloud all around me. I love to hear you say, "This is my beloved with whom I am well pleased." I am thrilled to follow the wisdom of your cloud. I am your handmaiden; use me!

Ezekiel 1:15-21

Luke 1:26-38

Psalm 91

THE JOY OF INTIMACY

For just one day of intimacy with you is like a thousand days of joy rolled into one! I'd rather stand at the threshold in front of the Gate Beautiful, ready to go in and worship my God, than to live my life without you.

Psalm 84:10 TPT

I am yearning to satisfy your longings! Come up to my temple courts by faith. Wrap yourself around my light-filled glory. I want to saturate you in the ecstasy of knowing me. I won't let you live without me; I draw your heart to me and hold you close. Don't be afraid to nestle in. I am a Father who loves relationships. Hallelujah! I love my children all around me. Better is one day in my courts than a thousand elsewhere. Love me with all your heart, soul, strength, and mind. Stay engaged with me, cling fiercely to my heart, and you will flourish, producing abundant supplies of fruit in every season.

My love is intoxicating and stunning from every viewpoint. All around me are rainbows, fragrances, songs, flashes of lightning, and my very nature's creativity. Run into my very center! For I am delightful in every way. You will taste and see that I am good and full of pleasure and fun. I am the King of the Universe. The beauty and joy of intimacy with me is for all to experience.

Father, I decree you are altogether lovely! I never want to live my life without you! Your joy and bliss delight me endlessly. I want to nestle in close enough to hear your heartbeat. I love our intimate relationship. Your loving kindness is worthy of all my adoration.

John 17:3

Psalm 43:4

Psalm 84:1-2

GOD REJOICES OVER YOU

The LORD your God in your midst, The Mighty
One, will save; He will rejoice over you with
gladness, He will quiet you with His love, He will
rejoice over you with singing.

Zephaniah 3:17 NKJV

Oh, beloved, I am inside your temple right in your very midst! I see you with the eyes of a proud Father. Together we are stunning, glorious, and holy. You are my innocent darling. I am so glad now that you are mine. I couldn't ask for a better companion to bring restoration to the earth.

We are united in heart-oneness, completely intertwined in tender love. We are together forever enraptured in our love song. Dance with me! I celebrate your royalty and worthiness. And I want you to know this—I am thrilled to be loved the same as you. I treasure your pursuit of our togetherness. So come running after me; come calling after me. I will show you that I will never leave you. Sing with me, walk with me, and talk with me. As my beloved child, I will pour all the riches of my Kingdom over you every day. Simply receive my grace.

Father, I adore our oneness! I never want to be alone again. In the stillness, your sweet love songs bless me over and over. I willingly give you all that I am forever.

Mark 12:30

John 17:20-26

Deuteronomy 31:8

THE FATHER'S DANCE

Engagement

Envision yourself in the middle of passionate worship, and you hear your Father calling your name. From the realms of heaven, he is extending his hand toward you and inviting you as his child to dance in the song of all songs. You smell the beautiful fragrances of his purity and holiness. Bliss! He is the kindest, most thrilling person you will ever meet. He is telling you all about being made for his glory. As you come near to him, ask him for the Spirit of wisdom and revelation to open the eyes of your heart. Ask him to show you around and to increase your spiritual sensitivity. Be curious. This is your home in the heavenly places, and he is opening up a new realm for you on the dance floor of heaven.

Turn on your favorite worship music. Dance, sing, and twirl around on the sapphire floors—the Father of Glory wants to dance with his child. Sense that he and his angels are flowing all about you. Oh, he rejoices over you without holding back. And he loves your free and undignified worship. Be ravished. Let love and grace flood your entire system as he becomes tangible and thrills your heart with the joy and ecstasy of experiencing his fatherly love. You have come up out of the wilderness leaning on him. He adores dancing with you and showing off your beauty to all of heaven. He is handing out new dancing shoes!

HUNGER AND THIRST

Blessed are those who hunger and thirst for righteousness, For they shall be filled.

Matthew 5:6 NKJV

Oh, how fortunate are those who desire and hunger after me. I will bless and nourish my beloved in every way. I want the cry of your heart to be "more of you, God, at any cost…there is none like you." If you are lovesick, nothing else will matter to you, and your food will be to do what brings me delight. We are one. My bride enjoys a complete satisfaction in her spirit that others know nothing about. I carry her right next to my heart.

The world will try to sway you, but the case is closed. I am flinging wide the doors to the pleasures of righteousness. I want to captivate, fill, and keep on filling you. You are truly my rose, the very theme of my song. Allow me to lead you in my footsteps on the highway of holiness. The potential of our divine partnership is limitless. I have so much to teach you about the ways of my Kingdom. I am releasing a Spirit of hunger right now.

Jesus, you are fabulously delightful. My heart is bursting with song for I am totally lovesick. I surely hunger and thirst for righteousness. I want more of you at any cost. You have made yourself so real that I experience you on every level of my being. It is my food to do your will and your pleasure!

Song of Solomon 2:1

Psalm 23:3

John 4:32-34

TRUTH MAKES YOU FREE

And you shall know the truth, and the truth shall
make you free."

John 8:32 NKJV

My heart is crying out for you to experience me: real encounters, authentic engagement, heart-to-heart. I am the truth. I am a genuine, living being, not just words in the Bible. I want to share my heart, my word, and my revelation light and to be known and experienced by you. I am alive and well and very much into face-to-face relationships. I will get real with you because I love you and want you set free! I already see and know everything about you. So come to me, and my truth will set you free.

The more time you spend with me, the more I will teach you how to recognize the lies. The enemy comes to kill, steal, and destroy, but I come to bring life. Sometimes deception has been sown into you for so long you don't even recognize it. But I am releasing to you an increase of discernment. I am also resetting your thinking to ponder on whatever is lovely, noble, and pure. I bless you to take your thoughts captive and replace them with truth.

Jesus, thank you for drawing me near to know you. I am wild over you! I want to experience you through face-to-face encounters. With all my heart, I want to discern lies from truth so I can replace them with the blessings of your intentions.

John 10:10

2 Corinthians 10:3-6

Philippians 4:8

GUSHING FOUNTAIN

A fountain of life was in him, for his life is light for all humanity. And this Light never fails to shine through darkness—Light that darkness could not overcome!

John 1:4-5 TPT

I am releasing an invitation to come to my fountain of life. I am in your center. Come and play until you overflow and there is no dry place left. It is a glorious cleansing light that shines through the darkness. Play like a child. The closer you get inside my heart, the more power, energy, and frequency you will find—vibrant and overflowing life and more life. I am your Light and stronghold, and I cannot be overcome! I never fail to shine and to love. My generous nature is to restore all who come. My bride, you have the same purpose.

You are called as sons and daughters to be a city on a hill. Full of light and life for all. Shine, my beauties, shine. When you dance and sing in high praise, you release the fountain of life inside of you. Light for all humanity. Gross darkness may cover the earth. But you will arise and shine for the glory of the Lord has arisen upon you.

And nations will come to the brightness of your rising. Your sons and daughters will come from afar. Cling to and hold fast to me because I am awakening the nations.

Father, I will play with you in your fountain of life. Teach me the way. Saturate me with light. I love your mysteries. Yes, show me! I want to rise up and shine before the nations.

Psalm 36:9

Matthew 5:14-16

Isaiah 60:1-3

LIBERTY

Now the Lord is the Spirit; and where the Spirit of the Lord is, there is liberty. But we all, with unveiled face, beholding as in a mirror the glory of the Lord, are being transformed into the same image from glory to glory, just as by the Spirit of the Lord.

2 Corinthians 3:17-18 NKJV

Beautiful children, your faces have been unveiled by my Son's work on the cross. You are in the Holy Spirit now, and there is freedom for you to come and behold me. I will miraculously transform you and shine you like a diamond in glory. Imagine I am blowing my sacred fragrances and spices in your garden. Receive all my blessings. I want your heart overflowing with fruit and precious and delightful gifts. Allow me to hold you close to my heart daily, and you will go from glory to glory.

Let us climb the high places. I am the God of the mountains! I fly free, and I release your wings to fly. Soar with me on the winds of ease. Let go of all that holds you back. You have a spirit that is limitless, glorious, and free. With our hearts entwined together, signs, wonders, and miracles happen all around us. I love your hunger for more. Keep looking, beholding, and treasuring me above all else. I love you, my child.

Father, I want more of the Holy Spirit. I thank you that he brings such freedom and miracles to all. But I want more. Start with me, Holy Spirit! Keep my eyes set on beholding my beloved in glory. I say yes to becoming your dazzling diamond and displaying signs and wonders with you!

John 14:12-14

Acts 1:8

Song of Solomon 4:16

_____

_____

_____

IMMORTAL LIFE WITHIN

*This truth is now being unveiled by the revelation of
the anointed Jesus, our life-giver, who has disman-
tled death, obliterating all its effects on our lives, and
has manifested his immortal life in us by the gospel.*

2 Timothy 1:10 TPT

Let the praises begin! I have obliterated death and manifested my Son and his immortal life inside you. Wahoo! He had the fullness of the deity living in him in human form. No truth could be more exhilaratingly powerful than this! You are complete now, thanks be to God. As Jesus is, so are you in the world. You have the opportunity to live a long and healthy life for you are my body and I am at your side. I have given you all that I am and all that I have. I have blessed you with my eternal life because I love you.

Limitless adventures are calling, and we have much to accomplish together, beloved. Yes, let us laugh and play in our imagination until we are ready to bring it on earth as it is in heaven. We will want to do this together daily as you choose life and run with the vision. I am a redeemer. I desire to redeem everything in your life and restore families, cities, and nations. You can do all things through Christ who strengthens you. You have my life, my heart, my power, my anointing, my love, and my mind. Run with me, my child. I bless you for creating life!

Father, I am exhilarated by your gift of immortal life within me! How can I ever thank you enough? Yes! I choose to live a long, healthy life of adventure. I want to run with your vision for my life. I can do this thing with you. What an honor, Lord.

1 John 4:17

Colossians 2:9

Habakkuk 2:2

I BELIEVE

*God is not a man, that He should lie, Nor a son
of man, that He should repent. Has He said, and
will He not do? Or has He spoken, and will He not
make it good?*

Numbers 23:19 NKJV

My child, I am confident in my promises to you as my beloved. They are all a delightful yes and amen. Search for them in my Word. Have faith in me because I am not a man, that I should lie. I am the creator and live in the realm of eternal truth. I see from the heavenly perspective of eternity. On every level, my intentions and purposes work for good. Even though you don't immediately see some of the answers to your prayers, believe I have a divine plan and timing. I know the best strategy for your eternal victory.

Take every lying circumstance that does not align with truth and cast that vain imagination out of your mind. It will not serve you. Refuse to contemplate negatives and stand firm in your faith with your mind set on heaven. Replace every lie with my truth, and thank me. Ask me to remove any doubt and unbelief you have about my promise, and I will. I want to saturate you in faith and glorious victory. You are who I say you are, you have what I say you have, and you can do what I say you can do.

Father, I believe in you! I am excited about your good promises and want to bring you glory. Let's run in faith together. I know you are not a man who could lie, and I will not live in doubt, unbelief, or compromise. I want to demonstrate the full shining of your truth in my life. Thank you!

Romans 8:28

2 Corinthians 10:5

2 Corinthians 1:20

73

THE RICHES OF LIFE

The thief comes only in order to steal and kill and destroy. I came that they may have and enjoy life, and have it in abundance (to the full, till it overflows).

John 10:10 AMPC

Ho! Everyone who thirsts, come and enjoy a glorious life with me. I am the creator of life, full of wonder, new every day. I desire to pour out so many streams in the desert, that the earth will be saturated in life-giving splendor. It will be an overflowing garden of Eden full of abundant supply. Life is to be enjoyed to the fullest and lived with passionate love. Delight yourself in me.

The thief has come to steal your life away from you. He will move you to eat from the tree of good and evil. But I already came and released the victory, so now you can choose the tree of life again. It's all about discovering your identity as my son or daughter, a royal family member. The real mystery is that the Kingdom of God is inside you, and you are invited to receive your entire inheritance from my riches in glory. Wahoo! I release explosive refreshing and life to you on every dimension.

Wow, Father, you are irresistibly fun and so full of life! Yes, I receive your outpouring today until I overflow in every area. I don't want to miss one bit of who you are and what you are so freely giving out. Father, what you have given me is astonishing, and I willingly give it to others.

Isaiah 55:1-3

Romans 8:31-32

1 Peter 2:9

BLOOD OF THE LAMB

They conquered him completely through the blood
of the Lamb and the powerful word of his testimony.
They triumphed because they did not love and cling
to their own lives, even when faced with death.

Revelation 12:11 TPT

Sold out and forgiven lovers! I am calling you to follow me as bold lions. Cease striving on your own and come after my jealous heart, forgetting what lies behind. My child, let go of the world. Arise and shine as a fearless warrior. Even when faced with death, my mighty beloved ones stood fast in my love. They held on by my glorious testimony and the blood I shed on the cross.

As my dread champion in the high courts of the Lord, release my glory, bringing heaven on earth. My friend, you were born for such a time as this to rebuild the old ruins from your position as a priest, king, and prophet. The enemy relentlessly steals, kills, and destroys my people. He creates havoc and chaos around the world. Enough is enough! Because of my powerful blood, you have been forgiven, healed, justified, cleansed white as snow, and given authority. I activate you now into your place in the body of Christ as a conquering wonder!

Jesus, I decree that I am an overcomer! I am all in and all out for you. God, I am a dangerous wonder in your army. Possess me fully. I conquer the enemy by the blood of the lamb and the word of my testimony. I will not love my life unto death.

Matthew 5:14

John 10:10

Isaiah 61:4

_____

_____

_____

GLORIOUS SONS AND DAUGHTERS

*The whole creation waits breathless with anticipa-
tion for the revelation of God's sons and daughters
... that the creation itself will be set free from slavery
to decay and brought into the glorious freedom of
God's children.*

Romans 8:19, 21 CEB

My beauties, the whole earth is groaning for freedom from death and decay. My sons and daughters, you carry this secret mystery of everlasting life
inside of you. Hidden in you is a treasure chest of my
limitless power, authority, and grace: Christ, the hope of
glory. Wahoo! God in all his fullness, endlessly overflowing his explosive life through you—free, radiantly alive,
and flowing fountains of eternal life.

For ages, the lost have been searching for the secret of
the fountain of youth. I am the elixir of immortality!
Ho! I freely give myself to my children. People, animals,
plants, and the whole creation want to be free from the
slavery of death. That is why they are yearning for you

to release redemption! You are made in my image and are no longer only human. You carry my resurrection power. Share my love and pour it out on the broken. The water that I give to you springs up into everlasting life. It bubbles up and overflows from you wherever you go. Freely you have received, freely give!

Jesus, I decree that I am a son/daughter of God. I drink of your fountain of living waters until I overflow and flood the earth with Zoe life. I release your blessings of hope and eternal life to the world! You will redeem this earth and bring it back to life through me.

Colossians 1:27

John 10:10

John 4:14

SPIRIT OF RESURRECTION

Yes, God raised Jesus to life! And since God's Spirit of Resurrection lives in you, he will also raise your dying body to life by the same Spirit that breathes life into you!

Romans 8:11 TPT

Darling children, I am overflowing with life! I raised Jesus from the dead. He was beaten and bruised and marred beyond comprehension. But I raised him back to life! I am God's Spirit of resurrection, and I live in you. I will raise and restore your body to life also. From the largest to the tiniest cellular system, I will thrill your body with new life. Boldly approach the throne of grace to obtain help, for Jesus suffered the same temptations as you, so I sympathize with your weaknesses. I will fill you with oil, and you will be fresh and flourishing all the days of your life. I work for the good of those who love me.

Drink of me, and gushing supplies of life-giving waters will spring up from your belly. Play in my everlasting fountain of life. I am extending my hand to you; will you take mine in yours? Come into my fountains right now and dance in the light-filled waters. I love to give generously to all. Receive with an open heart my resurrection power. Sing and rejoice like a child, and have faith in me. I can restore anything.

Holy Spirit, I believe you! I love to be raised to life in your resurrection power. Light, joy, love, and grace flood me as I dance in your fountains together with you. My every system flourishes in your divine supply. I am forever grateful for your holy life in me!

Psalm 92:14

John 4:14

Hebrews 4:15-16

MIRACLE FOUNTAINS

Engagement

Imagine yourself stepping into the mighty person of the Holy Spirit and invite him to step into you. Ruach HaKodesh is the breath of life, and he is breathing in and through you now. Breathe deep. He wants to thrill every part and every dimension of your being with new life. He speaks over your new creation reality. The old is gone, and you are brand new. As you delight yourself in the Holy Spirit, even now, he is filling you with power and taking you to higher and higher levels of passionate love.

As he walks with and talks with you, see ahead of you a beautiful fountain. He desires to take you to the heavenly fountains of living waters. Enter into the Kingdom as a child and come right into the fountains. They are fountains of resurrection power, light, and miracles; they will spring up all around you and bring you back to life. Play with the Holy Spirit and dance with him in the waters. You are meeting your miracle-working God! There is nothing too hard for him. Fling, splash, create, and play in the waters. Let yourself be wildly free. Let it soak every part of you in every dimension: the deepest part of your soul, your framework, your organs, your cellular makeup. Release a shout! Say, "I am a new creation. I am full of life and more life. I am whole and healed." Speak over your body. You are the best prophet in your life. This fountain penetrates your DNA—see it spinning with gorgeous, glorious light, healing the depths of your blood and generational line. Receive the Spirit of adoption and bask in oneness with the Holy Spirit. You are united in a place of great authority and are no longer required to obey the fleshly things that have tried to hold you down. You can soar on his wings. Just like a mother hen wants to cover her chicks, the Holy Spirit wants to protect you now under the shadow of his supernatural wings. You are healed and made whole.

_____

_____

_____

BEAUTIFUL EYES

His head and his hair were white like wool—
white as glistening snow. And his eyes were like
flames of fire!

Revelation 1:14 TPT

Lord Jesus, you are our chief among ten thousand! Alpha and Omega, the beginning and the end, we adore you! All of heaven and earth want to bless the lamb of God and sing of you forever. Darling of heaven, your eyes are beautiful and captivating, like flames of fire. They reflect the universe in all its glittering beauty. All creation is seen and known before your eyes of kindness and compassion. As your Holy Spirit, I gladly go forth in my aspect of seven Spirits from the throne, forever watchful, omnipresent, omnipotent, and omniscient.

Within your eyes, each son and daughter draws near to see a reflection of themselves. You are the very core of their sonship. You have blessed them with a glorious identity and inheritance. Capture them with your beautiful eyes, Jesus! Draw them with the fragrance of Christ. I release the pure in heart that will see God. Those who will keep looking, keep seeing, and keep discerning. As your Holy Spirit, I will be sure to lead them to your captivating heart.

Holy Spirit, I am so thankful for your ministry on the earth. I would love for you to draw me closer and closer into intimacy with the Lord Jesus! What a blessing to see into his eyes and find myself and know who I really am. When I find Jesus, I will find me.

Revelation 4:1-3

1 Peter 3:12

Revelation 5:6

UNRELENTING FIRE

*Fasten me upon your heart as a seal of fire
forevermore. This living, consuming flame will
seal you as my prisoner of love. My passion is
stronger than the chains of death and the grave,
all consuming as the very flashes of fire from the
burning heart of God. Place this fierce, unrelenting fire over your entire being.*

Song of Solomon 8:6 TPT

Children, jealously cry out for my seal of fire upon your heart. Nothing can stand in your way! Yearn for oneness! My blazing flame will consume you as my captive of love. I will not deny your request. Separation is an illusion. The veil has been torn, and I am breaking down every deception to the truth. Many waters will not quench my love for you. Join the eternal dance with the Trinity. Let the passion burn! Refuse to be led any longer by the flesh. Set your spirit in the lead, and you will find me again.

I am releasing an intense love fire on the earth. Place it over your heart. I am a jealous God. My burning heart will cause my children's spirits to ignite with passion again. Revival, restoration, and renaissance will sweep the land. Signs and wonders will be everywhere. All dry, cracked, hard ground will give way to my love!

Jesus, yes! Place your seal of fire upon my heart. I want it to consume me in living flames of passion. Make me your prisoner of love! Help me run right into the burning heart of God with total abandon. With all my heart, I choose to burn with passion until we are ultimately one!

Song of Solomon 8:7

Matthew 27:50-53

Acts 2:17-21

JESUS THE BREAKER

The breaker [the Messiah, who opens the way] shall go up before them [liberating them]. They will break out, pass through the gate and go out; so their King goes on before them, the Lord at their head.

Micah 2:13 AMP

In this world, all kinds of mountains stand before you. Mountains that you have to speak to faithfully, travel over, or go all the way around. But I am with you as your King and I go through the fire with you. I know every stumbling block in your way. Believe in me; my mighty arms will destroy what's coming against you and at the same time turn you into a mighty warrior. I am the breaker, the one who leads the way. Like a hammer, my word can break through even the most complex situation. I can get you to where you are going in the grandest style.

Before my horses and chariots of fire, the gates will swing wide. There is nothing impossible for me. I am releasing a breakthrough. So look for a suddenly coming your way. There is one thing you need: to seek my face in the Spirit and inquire in my temple. Linger in worship a little longer, my champion. Let the sound of your praise change the atmosphere! Stay in step with me as I break right through!

Jesus, you are my miracle working breaker! I am so grateful you are breaking through the hardest rock as I speak your word and dance with your Holy Spirit. I believe in you. And as I seek your face, you do not fail to perform your word!

Jeremiah 23:29

2 Kings 6:15-17

Psalm 27:4-8

LET IT OUT!

*If I say, I will not make mention of [the Lord] or
speak any more in His name, in my mind and heart
it is as if there were a burning fire shut up in my
bones. And I am weary of enduring and holding it
in; I cannot [contain it any longer].*

Jeremiah 20:9 AMPC

My child, you are my powerful voice to the world.
I declare you are bold as a lion! I will fill your
mouth with burning love. Forget about qualifying yourself. I only need one available person. Jump in and let me
out. In the quiet moments, you will hear my whispers.
I challenge you to say my words. Let's do this together.

Beloved, man cannot reject you if I accept you, and
I break the fear of man off of you right now. You are
accepted in the beloved. Step out by faith with that
word, and it will forever change someone's life. Your
faith pleases me, and I love your obedience.

I am a burning passion *within* you, championing your
cause. I can do far above all you ask or think from my

power within your core. Listen, world changer, I am the mentor of your dreams! I care about you and your destiny. Let nothing stop the call on your life. You are my firebrand, my torch, my blazing one!

Jesus, I will shout out what you want to say from the center of my being! I will let nothing stop me from saying what you have given me. No more will I hold you back. Lord, I set you free to create through me. Teach me to be your oracle!

Proverbs 28:1

Hebrews 11:6

Ephesians 3:20

THE NAME OF JESUS

*Lord, your name is so great and powerful! People
everywhere see your splendor. Your glorious majesty
streams from the heavens, filling the earth with the
fame of your name!*

Psalm 8:1 TPT

The fame of my name circumvents the universe forever! I am Jesus, Yeshua Hamashiach, Messiah and savior of the world. At my all-powerful name, every knee will bow. I rule and reign in the Kingdom of God in absolute supremacy. Glorious majesty, healing, and joy flow from my presence. At the sound of my name, the deer give birth! Whisper it, and demons will run in terror. Shout it, and everlasting doors and gates will open. My name creates, heals, saves, delivers, blesses, legally binds, and so much more.

I have given you my name as part of my covenant. Live your life embracing my heart, cling to, and look at me. If my words abide in you, ask me in my name whatever you desire, and I will do it. Rejoice in my desire for you to be powerfully loved. In my name, you will be hidden and find a safe and mighty shelter.

Jesus, I decree your glorious splendor is on display for all the earth to see. Oh, Jesus, I love to say and to use your name all the time! I adore running into it and asking for everything my heart desires. Thank you, God!

Philippians 2:10

John 15:7

Proverbs 18:10

YESHUA ON FIRE

Also from the appearance of His waist and
upward I saw, as it were, the color of amber with
the appearance of fire all around within it; and
from the appearance of His waist and downward
I saw, as it were, the appearance of fire with
brightness all around.

Ezekiel 1:27 NKJV

I AM a consuming living flame of burning love. A man at the center of the throne raging with fire. Clouds radiant with brilliant rainbows encircle me. I have no rival and captivate all. This all-powerful love consumes me with passion for YOU as the object of my desire. Come and enjoy my presence. You were born to worship in the beauty of my holiness. This sapphire throne is your inheritance.

We have a dance, you and I. A dance in my dazzling sanctuary that unites us together in oneness. It's filled with bliss and power and takes you higher and higher in ascension. Cry out like Moses for me to show you my glory, and I will reveal it to you. I want you here with me in my glory. I will saturate you with desire as you dance in my passionate fire!

Jesus, my majestic one! Make me the flame of your desire. I will dance with you in the fire. My heart burns for you and all your bright, fiery love. Close me in your cloud-filled chamber. I can't get enough of worshipping you! Show me your glory.

Hebrews 12:22-29

Ephesians 2:6

Psalm 149:3

TRANSFIGURATION

*And He was transfigured before them. His face
shone like the sun, and His clothes became as
white as the light.*

Matthew 17:2 NKJV

My children, this is a glorious promise for you. My Son, who revealed himself in brilliant splendor, opened the door. What a stunning revelation as he took his disciples up the mount of transfiguration. He moved into the Kingdom and shifted dimensions with so much power that the disciples could see it in the natural. In his brilliance, so many heavenly gates were swung open that even Moses and Elijah could be seen. Will you step in with me, my child?

I am closing in on the earth with my glory. It will open before me and before you. You will see your spirit manifest my light like never before. Those who are hungry for it will be transformed, transported, and transfigured. Let go of the old and come into the new. You are a brand-new creation with unlimited possibilities. Just like Jesus, you have the same capacity. Get hungry because I am going to astound the nations with transfigurations!

Father, I am so excited to be able to release your light on a level like Jesus. I want to display your glory too! I am one of the hungry ones. I desire to do everything just like Jesus. I am a true disciple picking up my cross and following after you.

Mark 9:2-8

Luke 9:28-36

John 14:12-14

BURNING HOT!

For our God is a holy, devouring fire!

Hebrews 12:29 TPT

I AM brilliant, all-consuming, and blazing with fiery love. Love devours every part of me. Heaven is filled with dazzling light and glory; nothing is dull here. My passionate love extends and brings everything to life, and it catches everywhere! Come and play in the fire, my darling child; let it consume, refine, and purge you. If you let me have my way, I will remove every question and doubt. I am an all-knowing and very good Father.

The church has become lukewarm, but I want her burning hot. I want God-chasers! Wild ones that are consumed with my embrace and move with my heartbeat. Let me release over you a baptism with a raging fire. Become my beloved on fire. Just like the seven Spirits are burning and blazing before the throne, that's where I have called you. To arise and shine with fiery colors and rainbows—clear, gorgeous radiance. Ask for my fire!

Father, give me fire! More fire, more fire! I want to be pure and passionate and moving with your heartbeat. I am so in love with you. Consume me in your glory fire. I want to arise and shine and be clear, gorgeous, and radiant. Again and again, fresh fire all over the earth.

Matthew 3:11-12

Isaiah 6:1-6

Song of Solomon 8:6-7

GLORY

*I have seen you in the sanctuary and beheld your
power and your glory.*

Psalm 63:2 NIV

I am Lord of all! Even the rocks will cry out before me.
Every heart will burn in worship and every knee will
bow, and every tongue will confess that I am Lord. They
will all see, and they will all know. Yes, I give sight, and I
give ear. I love my creation to know who I am in all my
glory. Because of my goodness, all will cry out: "Please,
show me your glory." Just like Moses, there will be a time
when all will want to see me face-to-face and for my
presence to go with them.

I am rolling out revelation after revelation from the sanctuary of my beauty and glory. Come up here. You are
my temple within and without. I reward those who seek
after me diligently.

I am your sweet nourishment, beloved healer, and very
great reward. The most profound thing you can long for
is my heart!

Jesus, I will seek for you diligently. I hunger for more of your stunning beauty. I want to see. I want to hear every single revelation of your power and your glory. Please put me in your courts right in the middle of all the myriads and myriads of angels. I am jealous to have more of you and you alone. I surrender the lust of this world to behold you in your power and glory. I praise you, mighty Lord!

Philippians 2:9-11

Exodus 33

Hebrews 11:6

LEAPING OVER MOUNTAINS

Listen! I hear my lover's voice. I know it's him
coming to me—leaping with joy over mountains,
skipping in love over the hills that separate us, to
come to me.

Song of Solomon 2:8 TPT

Listen, oh daughter of Zion, for an enchanting sound is in the air. It's the joyful sound of my voice. I have been singing your name and destiny since you were born. You are my delightful rose and the very theme of my song. When I come near, your heart will bloom passionately, and fragrance will fill the air. I leap with joy over mountains and skip towards you in love. I come in strength and beauty and power. I am infinitely more than your most outstanding request. And I can't wait to exceed your wildest imagination!

I am setting a table for us in the lush green pastures of heaven. Dip into the still and quiet waters where I will restore your soul. Open all your senses; taste the sweetness, smell the fragrances, and see that I am good. Your most blessed moments now will be to experience my glorious presence. It is this knowing me that brings eternal life. Will you take my hand and join me? Let nothing separate us. No little foxes are allowed—no fences, no hills, no mountains. Lay them all down.

Jesus, nothing can separate our love for each other: no fences, hills, or mountains. You are all I want! I hear my lover's voice calling to me. Together, we climb and experience the heights of heaven. Yes, Lord, exceed my wildest imagination!

Song of Solomon 2:1

Ephesians 3:20

Psalm 23:1-3

HEALING LOVE WITH JESUS

Engagement

You are sitting in a beautiful grass field with a gentle breeze blowing on your face. In this place, you feel tremendously safe. The sun is shining on you, and you've been here before. You feel love coming close to you. And it's Jesus is skipping across the mountain meadows coming towards you. You can feel his heart smiling and it's pounding with love, joy, and beauty. There is a definite song in the air. You know he is bursting with songs just for you. You belong to him and he jealously rejoices over you. And he opens his arms wide with great love and invites you into the best hug of your life. You are in awe of his presence around you, expanding and blessing everything with love. Even the grasses are swaying with love.

He is whispering to you: "This is the moment I have been waiting to tell you, oh how I love you." And you lean your head over onto his shoulder and ask him: "Lord, what do you love about me?" He starts to tell you everything he has been longing to say, that you are his beloved and his favorite. He is asking you gently to give him any hurts you carry. As you do this, you are able look into his eyes even more clearly. He is a healer through and through; his most profound nature is to help you heal. And over and over he is filling you with love, like waterfalls washing over you. As you are feeling lighter, now you notice the birds are singing around you. And the tenderness of Jesus' heart has touched you deeply in places where no one has ever touched you before. And he says, "If you need to cry, you can cry. And if you want to embrace me, you can because I am right here next to you and I am pure, holy, and safe; your heart is protected in my hands."

OVERCOMING JOY

*You have loved righteousness [You have
delighted in integrity, virtue, and uprightness
in purpose, thought, and action] and You have
hated lawlessness (injustice and iniquity).
Therefore God, [even] Your God (Godhead), has
anointed You with the oil of exultant joy and
gladness above and beyond Your companions.*

Hebrews 1:9 AMPC

Come on, enter my joy, child! I will gladly cover you and anoint you with the oil of joy. The life of a son of God is one of overcoming bliss and integrity, no matter the storms. Yes, you are now a brand-new creation. Glowing through you are all my virtues and you can dive into whichever one you need. All the fruit of the Holy Spirit is yours.

The truth is I am a happy God who is full of contagious joy and laughter! I laugh with hilarity at the plans of the enemy. He is no match for my best strategies. Keep your heart full of thoughts of me. If I dwell in your heart, and my joy is the size of the universe, how much joy would you have? Infinite! Swim in my heart of joy like an ocean, soak it up, and give it away. It is a most potent weapon. At the sound of your glorious laughter, strongholds will break, and demons will flee.

Jesus, I am laughing and drinking with you! You are JOY from head to toe; I will not contain it. I will let it out and send my laughter worldwide as the greatest weapon ever conceived! Strongholds will break, and demons will flee. I say yes to more of your JOY!

Psalm 2:4

Galatians 5:22-23

Psalm 59:8

SPIRITUAL BLESSINGS

*Every spiritual blessing in the heavenly realm has
already been lavished upon us as a love gift from our
wonderful heavenly Father, the Father of our Lord
Jesus—all because he sees us wrapped into Christ.
This is why we celebrate him with all our hearts!*

Ephesians 1:3 TPT

My beloved, you are loaded with every spiritual
blessing from heaven! Benefits of salvation, life,
health, provision, healing, wisdom, angels, everything
that pertains to life and godliness. They are my love gift
according to the riches of my grace. I satisfied all the
written accusations against you on the cross. You are
a partaker of my divine nature now. Since these blessings are yours, they take no effort or work on your part
to accomplish. All because of Christ, they are yours by
grace through faith.

Please close your eyes now and receive a gift I want to
give you. Imagine a box with gorgeous wrapping, rib-
bon, fragrance, and weightiness, and sit with me in the
quiet so we can open it together. I bless your eyes to see

by faith what is inside. Let me show you all my love, gifts, and blessings. My beloved, you must know I am a generous God with unsearchable riches. I release to you the ability to receive them, even under the pressures and trials of life. My storehouses are open to you, my darling. Come and experience my limitless abundance.

Jesus, I will receive every spiritual blessing! I want them all. I see the love gift you are giving me, Lord, and I accept it with open arms. Thank you, Father God, for your generous blessings. I am thrilled to live life with you.

Colossians 2:11-15

2 Peter 1:1-4

Deuteronomy 28:1-13

MORE DELIGHTFUL
THAN WINE

*Let him kiss me with the kisses of his mouth— for
your love is better than wine.*

Song of Solomon 1:2 NKJV

I am happy to smother you with joyous kisses until you can no longer take your eyes off me. In the purity of our first love, your heart will soar to the heights of heaven in intoxicating bliss. Oh, passionate ones—celebrate my love because it is better than wine! The holy and righteous kisses of my mouth awaken the sleeping to life. Oh Yes! Arise! I will never stop loving you. I came out of eternity with a gift of sacred love to give away. And with my redemption kiss, I will powerfully deliver you from your enemy.

You ravish me! Your surrender to me has captured my heart. Your new life will unfold like the fragrant petals of a rose. Give over entirely. In my mighty arms of love, I will tenderly heal every wound of your broken heart. The world is chaotic, but you will finally rest in my presence. I delight and care endlessly over you. You alone are my desire. I release you into the ultimate prize, the sacred romance of my heart!

Jesus, you thrill my heart endlessly. Every day is a new dawning of the sunshine of your love. You have awakened me to life with your kisses! Your love is intoxicating. I give over my heart and surrender to you in total trust. My prize is to have you, Jesus! You are my sacred romance.

Song of Solomon 5:16

1 John 4:8

Psalm 78:42

HOUSE OF GLORY

*But I know that you will welcome me into your
house, for I am covered by your covenant of mercy
and love. So I come to your sanctuary with deepest
awe to bow in worship and adore you.*

Psalm 5:7 TPT

Come with expectancy into my blazing throne room!
Enter with a heart full of faith, for there is nothing
I cannot do. Your thankfulness, adoration, and love for
me open the gates of heaven. And you CAN live here
in the beauty of my holiness and experience it all, my
child. You are welcome in the Spirit realm, and my place
is yours.

I long for nothing more than to have you in glory with
me. United together as one, I desire your joy to be complete. Let's be together in ecstatic worship and commu-
nion. Explode in the joy of my presence. I am dancing
in lovingkindness all around you. All the power of the
Godhead is in YOUR midst. We are together. In my
house, you are limitless. Test out the width, the length,
the depth, and the height of my love. On every side, I

have nothing but boundless love for you. Tell of all my wondrous works toward you, for I am a God of endless miracles and wonders.

Oh Jesus, what an invitation! Yes, yes, yes, in my worship, the gates of heaven will be thrown open wide. I am a gate too! My worship becomes a connection between heaven and earth. I will live in your house forever in union with you. Over and over, I am undone by your majesty.

Psalm 26:8

John 17:24

Ephesians 3:18

PRAISES TO THE BEAUTIFUL GOD

Hallelujah! Praise the Lord! How beautiful it is when we sing our praises to the beautiful God, for praise makes you lovely before him and brings him great delight!

Psalm 147:1 TPT

Break open the skies with your praises! Praise me in my holy sanctuary. Your voice is lovely, and your face is beautiful. There is no more separation. I have torn the veil. There is no love like yours. Throw open all your doors and gates. Let your voice trumpet through the heavens. It is beautiful to sing praises to me.

You glisten, shine, and sparkle as I adorn you in robes of praise. I anoint you with precious oils of gladness. You are no longer of the world. You are made for my gaze. Forever and ever, I delight in your victorious worship. I see your heart overflowing with love as you are caught up in my Holy Spirit, and it's thrilling. Keep soaring higher in freedom upon his wings of love. I want you here in my glory.

Jesus, I will shout and break open the skies for you. My voice is sweet to you. Our love songs light up the skies with victory and beauty. From now on, I put on my robes of praise and dance with all my might before you. I engage you face-to-face, my beautiful God!

Song of Solomon 2:14

Isaiah 61:3

John 17:13-24

RAINBOW GLORY

As the appearance of the rainbow in the clouds on a
rainy day, so was the appearance of the surrounding
radiance. Such was the appearance of the likeness
of the glory of the Lord. And when I saw it, I fell on
my face and heard a voice speaking.

Ezekiel 1:28 NASB

My incredible rainbows are the reflection of my beauty and my promise to you. I am glowing and luminous all the time in my joyful nature. I settle issues with my laughter. No enemy can overpower me. I am the victorious one! My joy overflows in colors, fragrances, and frequencies. Come on up, drink, and get yourself filled so you can pour out on the earth. No eye has seen, nor ear heard, nor the heart of man imagined what I have prepared for those who love me. I am gushing out gems and jewels of revelation like never before on earth.

Go after my presence. Practice sensing my being, my breath, my heartbeat. You will begin to train your awareness toward me to know between good and evil. I am with you also, right in your heart. Let me kiss your heart back to life with love. You can be with me in my glory, too! You can be in both places because I am Yahweh in heaven and Emmanuel on earth. I release to you eye salve and pure eyes to see. I declare radical God encounters over you!

Jesus, I want awesome God encounters like this. Give me eyes to see you in all your radiance and glory. I receive your gems and jewels. I drink in your beauty and allow your love to flow through me to rock my world. I want to fall on my face before you in ecstatic praise!

1 Corinthians 2:9

Hebrews 5:14

John 17:23-24

OUR RADIANT KING

*His radiance is like the sunlight; He has rays flashing
from His hand, And there is the hiding of His power.*

Habakkuk 3:4 NASB

Holy Spirit cries out: "Oh, bask in the sunshine of his love! Feel streams of radiant glory flood through him in all his beauty. On his shoulders is a government of peace that extends forever. All glory, power, and honor to the King of the Universe. One look at his many-faceted character is like a brilliant diamond sparkling in beauty. Gorgeous! Children, even his voice causes the deer to give birth as he blazes with thunder and lightning.

Who is this powerful King? He is the Alpha and Omega, the beginning and the end, the one who came to destroy darkness. Even now, he wants you to reach toward him for more. Give him everything, and he will devour it with light, with rays flashing from his hands, the hiding place of his power. He cries out to you, come to me, and I will give you rest and refreshment."

Thank you, Holy Spirit, Jesus, you are my majestic King, I want to bask in the sunshine of your love. Oh, how I adore you. I give everything over into your hands of lightning power. Make me sparkle like a diamond with many facets. Indeed you are more than I can imagine in grace, power, beauty, and humility. My heart is yours forever!

Revelation 4:1-11

Hebrews 12:22-24

Psalm 29:9

OVERWHELMED WITH DELIGHT

When I screamed out, "Lord, I'm doomed!" your
fiery love was stirred and you raced to my rescue.
Whenever my busy thoughts were out of control,
the soothing comfort of your presence calmed me
down and overwhelmed me with delight.

Psalm 94:18-19 TPT

There is nothing that can stop my enthusiasm for you. You are my dove hidden in the clefts of the rock; let me see your face and hear your sweet voice, beloved. Whatever situation you are in, call me, and I will come. I know all about your adversary, and it is my nature to protect and defend you. I am your personal Savior. I will liberate you even to the uttermost. Neither death nor life, nor angels nor principalities, nor powers shall be able to separate you from my jealous love. Have I not said it, and will I not do it?

I will yet fill your mouth with infectious laughter and delight you unceasingly. For in my presence is the fullness of joy. Set your mind on heavenly things, rich treasures, and the joys of heaven. I want you overwhelmed with delight! Refrain from being moved by what you see in the natural. Determine to set your focus on me, the author and finisher of your faith. I am your perfect peace.

Jesus, your love makes my heart skip a beat. You rescued me out of the worst situation, and now nothing can separate the two of us. I am blessed to set my mind on you. With you by my side, I will laugh at the things to come.

Romans 8:38-39

Song of Solomon 2:14

Psalm 5:11

ANGELS OF JOY

The angel of the LORD encamps around those who fear Him [with awe-inspired reverence and worship Him with obedience], And He rescues [each of] them.

Psalm 34:7 AMP

Brilliant angels surround you when you live in reverent worship before me. They will deliver you, protect you, and arm you. They are sent ones and will minister to you. And since they stand before my face, they excel mightily in the strength of my joy. You will sometimes get blasted, charged, intoxicated, struck with heaven's lightning, and be unable to stand when they are near. If you keep asking for more of me (Holy Spirit), look out because I will come like a mighty rushing wind and bring my angels with me.

I am opening your eyes to see that they are all around you. Like Elisha prayed to open his servant's eyes—you will look and see the hills full of my horses and chariots of fire surrounding you. Angel armies are being released in this new era like never before, and they will carry my joy. They will move at my word. They will take your seed and turn it into a 100-fold harvest when you believe. Trust me, they love being your friend! Just ask me, and I will give you angels of joy.

Yes, Holy Spirit, my Lord of Hosts! I want all the angels of joy! Wahoo! I want to be protected and delivered. I am so excited to meet and interact with the mighty angels around me. Thank you that they carry out your word faithfully when I believe!

Psalm 103:20

Acts 2:1-14

2 Kings 6:15-17

LAUGHTER

He will yet fill your mouth with laughing, And
your lips with rejoicing.

Job 8:21 NKJV

Yes, get ready! Wrap yourself around me, my beloved. Hold fast to me because I will fill you with laughter. I want your lips rejoicing with constant praises! When you get to know me and experience me, you will find your lost treasure. I am intoxicating, filled with delight, and hilarious! In my presence is the fullness of joy.

I want to hear your giggles, your laughter, your sweet voice. It is music to my ears. Think of a father whose child brings light and a merry heart to his home. It's healing to the spirit, soul, and body like medicine. Oh, the delight of a child full of gladness and lightheartedness! Children can laugh hundreds of times each day and it's always contagious! It draws angels, and everyone wants more! I prepare a table before you, and I will anoint your head with oil until your cup is overflowing. I am always about the overflow. They could no longer stand when the glory fell in the temple. Surrender fully, my child, and keep drinking.

I release upgrades to you today! I am pouring it out, and you will walk in new levels of joy as you receive by faith!

Yes, Lord! *Oh, Jesus, I wrap myself around you. You are indeed hilarious and so much fun. You take me to the heights of joy and laughter. You light up every cell in my body with medicine. Be my joy forever. My cup is overflowing because of your love! Pour it on, Papa God!*

Song of Solomon 1:1-4

Proverbs 17:22

Psalm 23:5

OVERFLOWING JOY

Engagement

Imagine that Father has invited you to his table, and the fullness of joy is in his presence. As you sit, you see him strolling towards you in the distance. As he gets closer, you can feel the King of Glory's joy, and it's contagious. You can see the smile on his face as he gets close. The Father is barely able to contain himself as he settles in at the table. He wants to fill your cup to overflowing with his Holy Spirit. Be intoxicated with his love, throw your arms around him, look into his eyes, and enter the fullness of his happiness.

His laughter is infectious. As the King, he sits in heaven and laughs and scatters the enemy. Let yourself be free to laugh with him. He will fill your mouth with laughter as he mixes his wine. He wants a child's full, free-flowing, uninhibited laughter to burst out of your mouth. It terrifies the enemy, and firmly settles the authority issue.

Today, he is breaking off anything that stops the power of your laughter. Ask him where you are positioned in Christ and if the enemy is under your feet. He wants you to know you are the head and not the tail, and you are above and not beneath. Ask him to tell you more. Throw off all the heaviness; he wants to sweep you off your feet. Delight yourself in him. Let go of the religious rules and regulations. Today is your day to laugh with abandon.

SAINTS OF LIGHT

*Giving thanks to the Father who has qualified
us to be partakers of the inheritance of the
saints in the light. He has delivered us from the
power of darkness and conveyed us into the
kingdom of the Son of His love.*

Colossians 1:12-13 NKJV

My beloved friend, give thanks for my master-
ful plan to redeem everyone through Jesus! You
are now in the Kingdom realms of love and glory. The
Kingdom is limitless, filled with the riches of wisdom,
and vast indeed. You are rightfully a saint of light with
an incredible inheritance. As an heir, you reign in life by
Christ Jesus.

Come up and soak in all the glory and light and be filled
again and again with my wonderful Holy Spirit. I will
release to you your divine purpose as you carry my hope
of glory to the world. Taste my good plan for you. My
beauty, Jesus erased the accusations against you. They
have been canceled and nailed to the cross. Jesus has

finished it all. Rejoice in your new identity as my son or daughter! You are free! You can now co-create from my realm of light and love.

Father, I am so grateful for your Son's display of power and mercy on the cross. I cherish my inheritance in the saints of light. I will come up, soak in glory, and listen to you endlessly telling me my purpose. I am so excited that you have wrapped yourself around me and we can co-create together!

Ephesians 1:17-19

Colossians 1:27

Colossians 2:12-14

ROYAL CROWN

*You will be a beautiful crown held high in the hand
of Yahweh, a royal crown of splendor held in the
open palm of your God!*

Isaiah 62:3 TPT

My beloved bride, you have been crowned with royalty. You are highly valued and treasured. Even God holds you up as a beautiful crown of splendor. Your light is dazzling and blinding, snuffing out the darkness. Every facet of your being is radiant, gorgeous, and full of life.

A crown describes your position of power well. My friend, your Father is a King. All authority in heaven and on earth was given to me. When you said yes to me, you entered a priesthood of kingly lineage, a holy nation, and a people belonging especially to God. I crowned you to minister before the Lord of the universe. It's your race now. You receive it from the abundance of my grace and as a gift of righteousness. There is no performance here! Your crown is a free gift; you can rule and reign on earth by it.

Delight in your royal priesthood! Like Queen Esther, you will come before the Father with your requests, and he will extend his royal scepter to you. Ask him, and declare your kingly decree, and light will shine upon your ways.

Jesus, I am adored by you as your beloved bride. My crown of splendor shines bright with royal authority. Like Queen Esther, I co-partner with my King. Thanks to you, I receive my gift of righteousness, and I rule and reign on this earth. I am held high in the hand of Yahweh.

Romans 5:17

Esther 5:2-3

Job 22:28

HIS PROMISES

The words and promises of the Lord are pure words,
like silver refined in an earthen furnace, purified
seven times over.

Psalm 12:6 NKJV

I uphold the earth with the word of my power. My words are full of remarkable purity, substance, promise, and life. Ha! They are literally containers of explosive power and quite dependable. I use them to frame up my desires like a house. They are foundations, walls, and ceilings—living and alive. They bring clarity to my wishes. I speak them with the breath of life and my Holy Spirit and send them forth, and they do not return to me void of my desire.

My promises are sure and solid. My word works effectively for those who believe. If I have given you a promise, I have sown it into your heart. When you receive it in rich, deep soil, it will produce a harvest—sometimes 30, 60, 100 fold. Ask with faith, and don't be tossed about by every wave in the sea. Work with my promise, ponder it in your heart, meditate on it, contend with it, speak it from heaven. Come to me with it, and we can make a plan for how to manifest it. I love you to have faith in me. Thank me and run with it by faith. Test it out by trying it. When you get a pure word from me, it's your blessing! All my promises are yes and amen!

Jesus, thank you! I love your astonishing and miraculous promises to me. By faith, I receive them and believe them. I declare I will see your pure words manifest in my life because they are solid, reliable, and trustworthy.

Hebrews 11:3

1 Thessalonians 2:13

Matthew 13:18-23

ADORNED

The city has no need for the sun or moon to shine, for the glory of God is its light, and its lamp is the Lamb.

Revelation 21:23 TPT

Behold my radiant city—the New Jerusalem! It is finished, my darling. It's built on a foundation of jewels and made of pure gold. Stunning in its beauty and glory. She pleases me like a bride adorned for her husband. There is no need for a sun or a moon. There is no need for a temple. Oh, it's all about my presence, my face! I am limitless and infinite in every way. Do you want all of me for all of you? I give myself away totally to you! I sacrificed my son, the darling of heaven, for you so that you would enjoy eternal life. Truly, my love is extravagant! Sing, my beloved!

Your hands are on the door, dripping with myrrh. Come into my chambers. Let my passionate love and light overwhelm and fill your heart. Over and over, I will fill you until your eyes are open wide and your lamp never goes out. Oh beloved, I want you here in my glory. My child, my child, I know of the heartbreaks in your life, and I will wipe away every tear.

Holy passionate Father—*Wow! I am stunned by your generosity and grandiose plans for the bride. How can it be? That I am one with you? Awesome infinite Father, I vulnerably open wide the door of my heart for you. I trust you to wipe away every trauma and tear as I lean on you.*

Revelation 21

John 17:24

Song of Solomon 5:5

LIGHT OF THE WORLD

*You are the light of the world. A city on a hill
cannot be hidden.*

Matthew 5:14 NKJV

Welcome to the bright and shining new day! Fresh light abounds. Throw open your windows. Breathe deep. You are the light of the world. Unmatched in selfless beauty, you are free to shine, so shine on. My darling, you are sensational in Christ.

Roses enchant the eye to behold them, so you will also attract the world. They will come from afar to your light and the brightness of your rising. Ravished by my beauty, they will come longing. When you share my love with others, I will bathe them in light and soften their hearts and hold them close. Sow seeds filled with light, and they will produce a harvest.

Darkness will cover the earth, but the Lord will arise over you. My light shines forth unobstructed, and of the increase of my government there will be no end. I am open, generous, and awesome to behold. I am the Father of Lights, continuously radiant. In our divine union and oneness, you are just as beautiful! Imitate your Father, my child. Arise and shine, for the glory of the Lord has arisen upon you.

Lord, I throw open all my windows and shine my light around the world. I am beautiful with you inside me. I will not keep you a secret, God. I shout about you from the rooftops. And the nations will come to the brightness of my rising!

Isaiah 60:1-3

James 1:17

1 Thessalonians 5:5

CHOSEN, HOLY, AND DEARLY LOVED

And he chose us to be his very own, joining us to
himself even before he laid the foundation of the
universe! Because of his great love, he ordained us,
so that we would be seen as holy in his eyes with an
unstained innocence.

Ephesians 1:4 TPT

Oh, my child, you are chosen, holy, and dearly loved. You are set apart now for my sacred purposes. Even before the universe's foundation, I intended to have you as my own. Let that word "chosen" sink into your very core. You are valuable beyond measure! Because of my great affection for you, it's official by decree—you have become mine. You are holy!

You have been made alive together with me. And you have been forgiven all your trespasses. Because you have been thoroughly washed and cleansed by my blood, you are now without flaw. Sparkling and innocent in my eyes. The accusations against you are wiped clean by my triumphant mercy, every last one. You are all fair, my love, and there is no spot in you. I have crowned you as royalty, my darling. And I choose to dance with you. Will you take my hand?

Jesus, it is my most incredible honor to be chosen by you! I cherish being one with you. I receive your love and forgiveness with all my heart. Yes! I am ordained and set apart for your holy purposes!

Song of Solomon 4:7

Psalm 103:3

Colossians 2:13-14

HOUSE OF WINE

Suddenly, he transported me into his house
of wine—he looked upon me with his
unrelenting love divine.

Song of Solomon 2:4 TPT

Oh, my delightful bride, on the clouds I ride! I will draw you away quickly from worldly concerns, and take you suddenly. Love me with all your heart. Let yourself soar on my wings of joy. I want to sweep you off your feet and take you to the banquet. Take my hand! You are invited to my house of wine into all the fullness of my Holy Spirit. In my presence is the fullness of joy.

It can be as simple as closing your eyes. I turned the water of the world into wine and love divine. Ascend with me to the heights of heaven. You are made to enjoy me. Delight! Let me look upon you and draw you into my heart. Captivated—breathe deep the passion in my eyes. You are completely protected and secure in my fortress of glory light. You are a chalice made for my beautiful Holy Spirit. Be intoxicated in the wine of the new covenant.

Jesus, *I decree that your love relentlessly pursues me until I am fully intoxicated. Even if I make my bed in the depths, you are there. In your house of wine, I will drink of your beauty forever.*

Psalm 16:11

Psalm 23:5

John 2:7-10

LOVE NEVER FAILS

Love suffers long and is kind; love does not envy; love does not parade itself, is not puffed up; does not behave rudely, does not seek its own, is not provoked, thinks no evil; does not rejoice in iniquity, but rejoices in the truth; bears all things, believes all things, hopes all things, endures all things. Love never fails.

1 Corinthians 13:4-8 NKJV

I rejoice over you, dearest child. You are my vessel of love. And oh, how I adore seeing my children bringing the truth of love to the earth. You have everything you need to be patient, kind, humble, truthful, faithful, hopeful, and persistent. Hope will explode out of you as I pour myself through you to the world.

I am a river of gorgeous love, bursting with fountains of life. I am releasing it now. All creation is groaning for the lovers of God to know their true power. You are my champions, full of grace and light. You shine with my delight, and you shine with my beauty. All of my characteristics are inside you. The world is waiting to be loved! They will come because of your ardent passion for me. And that love will never fail because I am moving through you.

Jesus, I want to flow with your love too! Thank you that I have all the riches of the Holy Spirit. I declare I am patient and kind, humble and persistent. I have you within me, yearning to love others every day. I am willing to feed your children; I give you away!

John 4:14

Romans 8:23-24

Matthew 14:16

A LOVE BLESSING

The Lord bless you and keep you; The Lord make
His face shine upon you, And be gracious to you;
The Lord lift up His countenance upon you, And
give you peace.

Numbers 6:24-26 NKJV

The Christian life is full of bountiful blessings. I bestow to my children precious love qualities and treasured love gifts. In my kindness, I will bless and keep you and guard you. I will make my face shine upon you. Come after me, my child. Pursue me. I love to be gracious, merciful, and compassionate. When I smile upon your life, you will know without a doubt that you are my delight. My blessings will chase you down!

The perfect gift from above is my death upon the cross. Those who believe can receive everlasting life and every redemption blessing. Salvation, healing, deliverance, and provision are a few of them. I make it clear that I live to give! I give you every spiritual blessing, everything I have, and all I am. Live out of the overflow of my generosity. As my priest, go now and release blessings to others. I send you to the nations to be a love blessing to my people. Reap a great harvest among your brothers and sisters.

Jesus, I decree that your blessings have chased me down! I am forever grateful for you, my beloved, and your work on the cross! Because I live in the overflow of your love, I am outrageously generous to others.

James 1:17

Ephesians 1:3

2 Corinthians 9:8-11

THE PERFECTION OF LOVE

No one has seen God at any time. But if we love one another [with unselfish concern], God abides in us, and His love [the love that is His essence abides in us and] is completed and perfected in us.

1 John 4:12 AMP

My very heartbeat is love, glorious love! It is my very essence. I loved you and drew you near me first. Now, you glow with my radiance. When you share with others, this rich passion increases exponentially. And you will find that I am right in the center of it all, creating and perfecting—a touch here and there.

Beloved, never stop the flow of your heartfelt passion. It is limitless inside of you. Let it splash out all around you. Like a river of splendor, it will overflow your gates and doors to the world. It will change atmospheres and melt the hardest of hearts. Imagine yourself blessing your friends or community. Jump in and let go and start today! You have so much to offer the world.

Together, let's go find someone who needs love every day. And freely give it away!

146

Jesus, I decree that loving on others is the joy of my life. It's a gift that keeps on giving. Every day I jump out of bed ready to give love away freely! I never want to close down my heart again.

1 Thessalonians 3:12

1 Peter 4:8

Jeremiah 31:3

THE JOY OF LOVING

Engagement

My friend, at his throne, Yahweh has a beautiful river that flows through the city called the River of Delight. He is inviting you to imagine and step into this river. It is flowing out of his throne like crystal clear waters. It's pure, holy, cleansing, healing, and filled with love and joy. As a child, come and play in the river. You can plunge your toes in and feel it flowing over you. It's alive with the Holy Spirit and is giggling with laughter. Now, go a little deeper. Feel the velvety smoothness of the glory water. It is full of his shalom peace. You can relax every inch of your body in the vast expanse of this water and let it carry you.

Envision that he has given you your very own gushing fountain of the Holy Spirit. It's living water that springs up into a fountain of eternal life. Keep expanding your river. By faith send it to overflow from you to love the world; a limitless river of love flowing out of you as you pray to heal your family, friends, city, and nation. Everywhere you go, you get to love and bless others with

Holy Spirit! It's a joy to love and see God do miracles through your saturation level. Let it splash out of you everywhere; you are a gate of heaven as you pray. Ask him who you can love today. Open your doors and gates and bless the world with the Holy Spirit.

I AM THE GOOD SHEPHERD

*The Lord is my best friend and my Shepherd. I
always have more than enough. He offers a resting
place for me in his luxurious love. His tracks take me
to an oasis of peace, the quiet brook of bliss.*

Psalm 23:1-2 TPT

I am passionately in love with you! I AM the good
Shepherd who has laid his life down for you. I long
to be your best friend and companion. There is a resting
place for you in my luxurious love. I know the world is
full of chaos. But I want to lead you to perfect tranquility. Among the streams of glory, I have still and quiet
waters of bliss where I will heal your soul. I will take you
there now!

Come away with me. Let the world go. I am inviting you
to lie down in green pastures in heavenly places. Smell
the fragrances and see the glorious colors. I am calling
your name. Do you hear it? Rest in my arms. I will quiet
you in my love. I will take good care of you and lead
you into abundant supply. As your best friend, I long to
look into your eyes and thrill your every desire. Be mine!

I have come for you, leaping upon the mountains and skipping upon the hills.

Jesus, I decree you are my best friend, my Shepherd, and my paradise. You absolutely sustain me and heal me with your everlasting love. My King and my beloved, my heart soars when you look into my eyes. Wrap me around your heart. There is none as magnificent as you!

John 10:11-16

Song of Solomon 2:8

Zephaniah 3:17

TRUSTWORTHY

*Commit your way to the Lord [roll and repose
each care of your load on Him]; trust (lean on,
rely on, and be confident) also in Him and He
will bring it to pass.*

Psalm 37:5 AMPC

Whatever your goal is, fill your days with superb delight in me. Roll everything onto me. Let it all go. Yes! Invite me to every minute. Little one, yoke yourself to me. I know life can get heavy if you are doing things on your own. Let's be together! I am right beside you, ready to lift that 1,000 lb. weight. To me, your life goals and pressures are light as a feather. Become like a little child, and let Daddy carry it for you.

Let everything float away in my river of everlasting life as you bask in me. Spirit to spirit and breath to breath, we are to be together. Let your faith soar when we are this close and responsive to one another. Lean on me. I am entirely reliable and trustworthy. Before you know it, you are in my arms, and your goal has come to pass. You see, my abilities are supernaturally far above all you can dream, think, or imagine.

Jesus, I decree that you are delightful and trustworthy in every way. I want to run with you and commit everything in life to you. Out of the goodness of your heart, you will bring my desires to pass.

1 Peter 5:6-7

Matthew 11:28-30

Proverbs 3:5-7

_____

_____

_____

THE GREATEST GIFT

This is the message which we have heard from Him
and declare to you, that God is light and in Him is no
darkness at all.

1 John 1:5 NKJV

I was born from above, my beauty. I entered the world as the light that would give life to men. I revealed to all that Yahweh is my Father. We were face-to-face before time began. I am the express representation of his image. The Father of Lights! A loving Father who gives good gifts.

We have always wanted to walk in the cool of the garden with you. To love, bless, make you fruitful, and give you rest. Our light reaches into the darkest recesses and brings things back to abundant life. Take my hand, my beloved. You have the power to experience me right now. When you choose me, the Father will give you to me, and nothing can snatch you out of my hand. Gorgeous child of light, you were the delightful joy set before me as I laid down my life. Rejoice, I say! My great love gift reconciles you back to the eternal life of your Heavenly Father.

Jesus, thank you that you came to rescue all of us back to the light of the Father. I experience your sweet love right now. May all your suffering on the cross raise us to the fullness of our relationship with our heavenly Father and seat us together with you.

James 1:17

Genesis 1:27-28

John 3:16-17

_____

_____

_____

WONDERFUL WAYS

"For My thoughts are not your thoughts, Nor are your ways My ways," says the Lord. For as the heavens are higher than the earth, So are My ways higher than your ways, And My thoughts than your thoughts.

Isaiah 55:8-9 NKJV

I am inviting you to a life of delightful awe and wonder. Come to me, and I will give you rest. Let's drink the water of life freely. Why spend money on what is not bread? I have made you an everlasting covenant of love. My heart aches to hold you in the glory realm and draw you into oneness. The ways of the Kingdom far surpass the earth, so seek my righteousness first, and I will add all the rest.

My counsel is wonderful, my peace passes understanding, no one can overcome my might, and my fatherhood is everlasting. The cloud of witnesses in heaven are cheering for you to learn to live from Zion. There will be no end to the increase of my government and peace. Ardently desire me! I am inviting you; my word will not return to me void. You are mine. And I am yours. Together, we will create a whole new world.

Oh Lord, I love you! Yes, I am hungry for you and your kind of life. This world is fallen, and nothing satisfies like you. I want to learn to live from glory and drink freely of your living waters. Being constantly aware of your stunning presence is my goal. I jump at the chance to co-create this world with you, Father. Bless you!

Isaiah 55:1-2, 11

Matthew 11:28-30

Isaiah 9:6-7

COME TO MY HOUSE

So, you are not foreigners or guests, but rather
you are the children of the city of the holy ones,
with all the rights as family members of the
household of God.

Ephesians 2:19 TPT

Come, run through my halls! With Jesus in your heart, you have the keys to my house. You are free here, and my doors are open wide. I am ringing the welcome bells. There is rejoicing in the presence of the angels of God over one who gets saved. Dear one, your heart is my desire. I will bestow the greatest gifts of grace and kindness upon you.

As my child, you have free access to the throne of grace. My presence is your very great reward. I will set you in a high place of protection, safe and secure before my face, so delight in me as your beloved. And every time you pray, I will answer your cry for help. You will be satisfied with my abundant life and my favor towards you. I want you to enjoy all the benefits of my salvation. Beloved, I want you as my friend!

Oh, Father, thank you for your plan of salvation. I love having Jesus in my heart, and now I have so many privileges as your child I can't count them all. Thank you for welcoming me into the family of God. Oh, what great saints surround me. Thank you that my heart is precious to you too. I love that you adore me and want me to be your friend!

Luke 15:10

Hebrews 4:16

Psalm 91:15-16

THE ULTIMATE SAFETY

*Yahweh himself will watch over you; he's always at
your side to shelter you safely in his presence.*

Psalm 121:5 TPT

I am roaring my love from Mount Zion! Let the enemy
scatter. I thunder from heaven over my children—as
a lion-hearted Father. Have no fear, my darling, for my
voice breaks the cedar trees and shakes the wilderness. I
will bless you with peace. I see around you on every side,
there is nothing hidden from me. Snuggle close with me.
If I am for you, who could possibly be against you?

Enter my rest and stay steadfast in your love for me.
Breathe in my comforting love. I will never let you go.
Fling wide your gates and let go of every lie that has
become a stronghold. My perfect love will cast out every
fear, and I will wash you with waves of glory. Let's go
swim in them even right now. Refrain from getting
caught up in the battle of the mind. Stay clinging to my
wondrous presence. Turn into your heart and see that
I am already seated there on my throne of sovereignty,
adoring you incessantly.

Wahoo, Father! *Roar over me with your voice that shatters the cedars! I love your lion-like jealousy over me. There is nothing more wonderful than being cherished in your eyes and swimming in your waves of glory. I gladly surrender my heart so I can enter your confident rest.*

Psalm 29

Romans 8:31

Hebrews 4:9-11

INNERMOST CHAMBER

See how his hands hold unlimited power!
But he never uses it in anger, for he is always holy,
displaying his glory. His innermost place is a work of
art— so beautiful and bright. How magnificent and
noble is this one— covered in majesty!

Song of Solomon 5:14 TPT

I hold in my hands magnificent power. Yet I never misuse it because I am lowly and gentle of heart. I am calling you, my darling, into my innermost chamber. Come and shut yourself in. It's a place of exquisite purity, love, and light. My light will bring you life, healing, wholeness, and truth. Bask in me! Rejoice in me! Let my diamond-like radiance soak you through. I want you to experience my goodness on every level: spirit, soul, and body. Throw open all of your senses. Open every gate and every door. My heart is bursting with lavishing love.

Like looking in a mirror, let my true beauty be your reflection. My character is flawless and on display for all to experience. I am the truth, so wrap yourself around me. Nothing pleases me more than to see my children walking in the truth. When you feel confused, be diligent to renew your mind with truth to illuminate your path. My light will brighten your heart.

Oh, Jesus, I will bask in you! I want my innermost place to be a work of art like yours. You are supremely powerful and yet make yourself so approachable to me. I love your majesty and your tender gentleness. Thank you for helping to make my heart as beautiful as yours.

2 Corinthians 4:6-7

Matthew 11:28-30

Psalm 24:7

RHYTHMS OF GRACE

Are you tired? Worn out? Burned out on religion?
Come to me. Get away with me and you'll recover
your life. I'll show you how to take a real rest. Walk
with me and work with me—watch how I do it. Learn
the unforced rhythms of grace. I won't lay anything
heavy or ill-fitting on you. Keep company with me
and you'll learn to live freely and lightly.

Matthew 11:28-30 MSG

I am shouting from heaven: it's all about a relationship with me! Following formulas will not satisfy your heart. Come and get away with me, and you will find your life. Take time for our love. I am jealous for you. Taste the sweetness of my kindness, feel the comfort of my arms around you. Fling back into my deep tranquility. I won't weigh you down with heavy burdens. But I will teach you to live freely and to focus on your unique calling.

I will bring you into a revelation of my rhythms of grace. Toiling and striving are not from me. I will make you lie down in the green pastures of glory. I will care for and shepherd you and lead you into a life of divine favor and unsearchable riches. No good thing will I withhold from you. Cling to me, stay hungry for me; I will answer your prayers. My many benefits are like a landslide for your support. You were born for real life, real zest, and absolute freedom!

Jesus, thank you for grace! I feel your arms around me and your heart beating passionately. You are so majestic, my chief among ten thousand. Whenever I realize I am striving or toiling, I will return my heart to you and rest in your lovingkindness and favor. Lead me, my beloved King!

Psalm 23

Galatians 3:13-14

Psalm 103:1-2

SURROUNDED BY PEACE

Perfect, absolute peace surrounds those whose
imaginations are consumed with you, they
confidently trust in you.

Isaiah 26:3 TPT

Oh, that I would captivate you completely! Let your hunger and thirst drive you right into my peaceful paradise. Minister to me, engage me constantly by abiding in my heart in the quiet. I love to breathe with you and draw you deeper. Honor me always, and you will find absolute peace surrounding you. I will miraculously lift you out of every circumstance as we commune together. Let my wrap-around presence absorb your imagination. I will expand your capacity every day. I love to be loved, and I will comfort you in my arms. Set your mind on the things above, for in my glory, the atmosphere is indeed perfect peace.

Let's define shalom peace: It contains wholeness, completeness, harmony, health, and safety. Release it over your whole spirit, soul, and body like a river. Declare order as a priest of the Most High God. My word does not return to you void. You rule and reign as a king in my realm. Let nothing break your focus, keeping your eye single. I have called my children to be seated in luxurious rest. Enter my rest and bask in new levels of trust. You are safe here, face-to-face with me.

Prince of Peace, I love you! I will continually commune with you and receive your wrap-around-peace every day. I pray for new hunger, focus, trust, and eyes to imagine you before me always. I want to enter your luxurious rest!

Psalm 34

Philippians 4:5-8

Hebrews 4:3,9-10

HIS RESTING PLACE

He offers a resting place for me in his luxurious love.
His tracks take me to an oasis of peace near the
quiet brook of bliss.

Psalm 23:2 TPT

Every chamber of my heart is beating with serene tranquility. Come, experience my heart, beloved. I want you to close your eyes to the worldly distractions, and melt in my peace. You will find still water you can step into. It's healing, refreshing, and full of life. Oh, allow it to wash over you and roll over you sweetly. Let it soak into your bones, cleansing away all that's not of me. Sink to the depths of rest; love is luxurious here. There is no want in the green pastures of my garden. My presence is all you need.

I will restore your soul. I am washing through and loosening all the debris, loving you repeatedly. Set your mind on the things above where I am seated. Always go deeper in my love, plumb the very depths, the height, the breadth, and the length of it. You will never find the end of me, beloved, and I will lavish you forever. I want to delight you with ecstatic encounters and keep you always longing for more. Fling yourself into my limitless tenderness. There is no match for my love.

Oh Jesus, you always leave me delighted and wanting more! You will give me an oasis of peace as I plumb the depths of your heart. I set aside time to sink tangibly into your brook of bliss. When I do, my soul is wonderfully satisfied and restored.

Colossians 3:1-3

Song of Solomon 6:2

Ephesians 3:14-19

BROOK OF BLISS

Engagement

See Jesus before you. He beckons you, "come to me, all who are weary." In his green pastures, he will make you lie down and rest. Receive his perfect peace that passes all understanding. Run your hand across the soft grass. There is no hurry here. There's a brook of bliss where he wants to restore your soul. Let yourself float in its gentle peace. Let him saturate you. Immerse yourself in the depths of his heart. Sink deeper into the river. He will wash you and cleanse your heart until nothing is left but love. My beloved, entwine yourself around him. Ask what his peace is like. Let it center you in such rest and grace that you feel weightless. He says: "I have finished the work; your only task now is to enter my rest."

Let him wash through your soul, purifying, healing, restoring, and bringing you back to life. Every stronghold is being removed that is not of him. Embrace him closely, and let him give you all you can drink until your heart overflows. Breathe in his love over and over. Ask him to show you that he created you to carry his glory.

Thank him for your life. Keep resting, soaking, and receiving all he wants to pour out over you. Let him lavish you in the depths of rest. When you come to his table, he will anoint you with the fragrance of the Holy Spirit. Smell his perfumed oil flooding over you. See if he has a gift for you. Savor his delicious feast even when your enemies dare to fight. His goodness and mercy will follow you all the days of your life.

DIVINE HELPER

And I will pray the Father, and He will give you another Helper, that He may abide with you forever—the Spirit of truth, whom the world cannot receive, because it neither sees Him nor knows Him; but you know Him, for He dwells with you and will be in you.

John 14:16-17 NKJV

Holy Spirit is his name! Divine brilliance, righteousness, and reassuring comfort are his attributes. He will be your helper and lead you into all truth. He loves you outrageously and knows you intimately. His attitude is filled with limitless hope, expectancy, and joy! Be sure to lean on him in times of adversity because he is acutely aware of the enemy's schemes. You have no worries with Holy Spirit; he is large and in charge. He is incredibly jealous for God's children and hovers over them constantly.

Never in your wildest dreams could you imagine companionship like this. Holy Spirit will free you, love you, cleanse you, fill you, and keep you. In every dimension and in every way that you need help, Holy Spirit will be there. He will shine his light and reveal every hidden thing for you. Remember to be still and know that he is God. His unlimited blessings will chase you down if you make yourself available and listen to his still, small voice!

Holy Spirit, wow! I am so grateful the Father has given you to me. Not a day goes by when I don't need your brilliant help. I love you dearly, Holy Spirit! You are my joy, my delight, my best friend, my freedom, my helper, and my confidant. I am forever yours!

2 Corinthians 3:17

James 4:5

1 Kings 19:11-13

WISDOM AND REVELATION

*I pray that the Father of glory, the God of our Lord
Jesus Christ, would impart to you the riches of the
Spirit of wisdom and the Spirit of revelation to know
him through your deepening intimacy with him.*

Ephesians 1:17 TPT

I want my bride to experience divine union with me.
My heart yearns jealously for intimacy. I am not one
bit religious, and my heart beats for face-to-face relationships. Come explore my heart. Ask for the riches of
the Spirit of wisdom and revelation! I am crying out in
the streets to those who want deep and personal insight.
Dive for revelation and secret mysteries. Throw open
every gate of your senses to know me. You will taste and
see that I am good.

This is only the beginning. For eternity, you will be
experiencing sweet and glorious intimacy with me.
Come and receive your inheritance's precious pearls,
gems, and treasures. Oh my goodness, my Holy Spirit
wants to lead you, so follow him. I am all around you
in many ways; even if you don't feel me, I am there. In

the stillness of your breath, I will teach you the ways of my glory.

Jesus, I receive all the riches of your Spirit of wisdom and revelation in the knowledge of you. I abide in the secret place of your mysteries. I breathe in your tender lovingkindness. Precious one, I trade all my crowns for more intimacy with you!

Psalm 25:14

James 4:5

Psalm 34:8

LADY WISDOM

When wisdom wins your heart and revelation breaks in, true pleasure enters your soul.

Proverbs 2:10 TPT

L ady wisdom comes from above to bring you godly gifts. She has in her hand living understanding. And when she wins your heart, look out! Revelation will flood into your life. Nothing can surpass the wise, joy-filled, and practical ways of my Kingdom. Wisdom holds the mysteries of righteousness, and she wants to impart them to you. Cry out for wisdom! Reverently fear and adore the Lord, for it is the beginning of wisdom.

The wisdom that comes from above is pure, peaceable, gentle, willing to yield, full of mercy and good fruits, and has no favoritism. Cling to wisdom, and you will learn to live life to the fullest. There is no problem wisdom cannot solve. You will dance in delight over my wisdom, and my knowledge will be sweet to your soul. Rejoice, I say! Rejoice! I release to you a wise and understanding heart; there will not be anyone like you or before you, nor shall any like you arise after you. I am committed to championing you, my beloved.

Holy Spirit, help me live life to the fullest with Lady Wisdom. I run with your heavenly wisdom and no longer lean on my understanding. I have a wise and understanding heart like Solomon. I wait at wisdom's gates daily!

Proverbs 9:10

James 3:17

1 Kings 3:12

IN THE SPIRIT

God is a Spirit (a spiritual Being) and those who
worship Him must worship Him in spirit and in
truth (reality).

John 4:24 AMPC

My Spirit is in your next breath. Breathe deeply—he will thrill and quicken you with fresh and new life. Holy Spirit brings my word and life. I placed you in the Holy Spirit just like you are in me. When you are inside the Holy Spirit, you are in true worship. And what a beautiful place that is to honor. John the beloved was "in" the Spirit on the Lord's day. Even as he breathed, he was caught up into the glorious throne room of heaven.

My Spirit is a consistent breath of love and flows like a river of life, springing into everlasting waters. His baptism is one of passionate fire and power! Dive deep into that fire and power. He is an omnipotent, omniscient, and omnipresent God at the center of the universe; he rests on and in you. My beloved friend, Holy Spirit, is perfect righteousness, peace, and joy.

Jesus, I treasure your beloved Holy Spirit. He carries such power and resurrection life. He embodies omnipotence on the earth. I want to be caught up into the throne room with all my heart. I love you, Holy Spirit!

Revelations 1:10

Revelation 4:1-5

John 4:13-14

POWER AND ABILITY

But you will receive power and ability when the
Holy Spirit comes upon you; and you will be
my witnesses [to tell people about me] both in
Jerusalem and in all Judea, and Samaria, and
even to the ends of the earth."

Acts 1:8 AMP

Hold up your heart to me and expect. Get excited! I am going to baptize you into my burning heart of love. I am going to fill you with explosive dunamis power! Let your heart soar with the thought of it. I AM with you. You will be seized with power, overwhelmed, saturated, and filled. And the Holy Spirit will rest, settle down, and dwell with you. I won't leave you orphans!

When you are full of my love, share about Jesus Christ, telling everyone about him. I am commissioning you to go and make disciples but not with man's wisdom—with a demonstration of power. Spirit-led miraculous power, love, ability, abundance, might, and strength. As my bride, I give you everything I have to use for your mission. Together, we will run to the harvest! I am releasing it now.

Jesus, I receive every ounce of the Holy Spirit you pour out on me! I share the love of your fiery overflow around the world. I walk in the supernatural power of signs, wonders, and miracles. Use me, God!

Luke 24:49

Matthew 3:11

Mark 16:15-20

_____

_____

_____

OUTPOURING OF THE HOLY SPIRIT

And it shall come to pass in the last days, says
God, That I will pour out of My Spirit on all flesh;
Your sons and your daughters shall prophesy,
Your young men shall see visions, Your old men
shall dream dreams.

Acts 2:17 NKJV

Since the cross and ascension, the Holy Spirit has been pouring and flooding and splashing his Spirit ocean of love everywhere. He gushes with miracles. He is a dynamo of power, might, and signs and wonders—like Holy Dynamite! Many appear to be besides themselves and drunk with wine. But it's the wine of the Holy Spirit. And in his presence is the fullness of joy, and at his right hand there are pleasures forevermore. Rejoice! He will ravish your heart and delight you endlessly.

Your sons and daughters, both men and women, will prophesy, see visions, and dream dreams. His supernatural power throws open spiritual eyes and ears. He comes bearing gifts. He turned the world upside down at Pentecost and he is still doing it today. The mighty Spirit's whirlwind of love changes everything. He wants to encounter you right now; so lean back and let him saturate you with love and power.

Jesus, I decree that you are filling me with more of your Holy Spirit. He is my dynamite! Fill me without measure! I hunger and thirst for his joyful and ravishing presence. My sons and daughters will prophesy, see visions, and dream dreams.

John 4:13-14

Psalm 16:11

Acts 2:41

SEVEN BLAZING TORCHES

And pulsing from the throne were blinding flashes of
lightning, crashes of thunder, and voices. And burn-
ing before the throne were seven blazing torches,
which represent the seven Spirits of God.

Revelation 4:5 TPT

I walk among the seven blazing torches of LOVE. I am
at home here with all the flashes of lightning, thunder, and voices. The seven Spirits of God are radiantly
burning and full of courage and might. They are a wildfire of passionate love and they desire to pour it all on
you. Trust me, they want to light you on fire! Learn to
surrender and make yourself a living sacrifice before the
altar at my throne. Put your heart on my altar of love to
purify yourself daily, and my fire will fall.

Charged with bringing my children up to full maturity,
the seven Spirits carry the Holy Spirit's mission on the
earth. They will serve you with the utmost loyalty as the
Holy Spirit directs them. They will counsel you with
excellent strategies to become a mighty warrior, and give
you extraordinary wisdom and perfect understanding.

Ask them to lead you into the blessings of profound intimacy with the Lord so you may gain great favor, mysteries and knowledge. Knowing him is eternal life.

Jesus, thank you! I want to meet the seven Spirits of God. They must be incredible. Help me put my heart on the altar daily to be holy. Help me to surrender to the seven Spirits so they can tutor me into the full stature of Christ.

Isaiah 11:2-3

Romans 12:1-2

Romans 8:14-23

PRAYING IN TONGUES

Holy Spirit takes hold of us in our human frailty to empower us in our weakness ... at times we don't even know how to pray, or know the best things to ask for. But the Holy Spirit rises up within us to super-intercede on our behalf, pleading to God with emotional sighs too deep for words.

Romans 8:26 TPT

I have a fabulous gift for you! If you want to see signs and wonders, this is for you. My Spirit carries this gem to every believer. And all you have to do is to desire it and give it a go. It's called a heavenly prayer language. And I love for my children to allow the Holy Spirit to pray through them. When you don't know what to do, my Spirit will rise within you and help you in your weakness. He searches out the best things for you within God's perfect will, even praying sometimes with emotional sighs too deep for words.

It will not make sense to your mind, but the Holy Spirit is infinitely beyond it. Tongues work in the unseen realm, the eternal realm that created this one. This language of light makes containers for my words of power. Believe that my Spirit is super-interceding for your miracles. Fill my ears with it today and pray it unceasingly.

Jesus, I truly desire the Holy Spirit today! By my free will and faith, I choose to speak in his powerful language of tongues. I want the Holy Spirit to super-intercede for me. I receive my miracle prayer language and pray it daily, amen.

1 Thessalonians 5:17

Jude 1:20-23

Mark 16:17-18

187

SUBMERGED IN LOVE

Those who repent I baptize with water, but there is
coming a man after me who is more powerful than
I am. In fact, I'm not even worthy enough to pick up
his sandals. He will submerge you into union with
the Spirit of Holiness and with a raging fire!

Matthew 3:11 TPT

I can imagine nothing more fun than baptizing you into my raging, fiery love. Oh my goodness, what a gift to be in union with the Spirit of Holiness. I want you going under over and over again. Leave no stone unturned. My glory will consume you until you become a blazing flame. Passionate lover, cling to my heart and run with me in your identity as a son of God.

The brighter you get, the more dangerous you will be. I destroyed the enemy with the breath of my mouth and the brightness of my presence. Keep coming back for more fire so you can shine bright. You become indomitable saturated in my presence. Play, play, play with me in all my power. Your spirit loves it! Let go of the old religious ways; there is no more veil. Enter as a child, and you will come right in. I am releasing the four winds to increase the fire; catch it!

Jesus, baptize me over and over again in your fire. Make me a wildfire! I want to be dangerous to the enemy too. Soak me with your fire and set your winds loose on me. May the fire catch everywhere I go!

Luke 12:49-50

2 Thessalonians 2:8

Matthew 18:2-5

COME, HOLY SPIRIT

Then all at once a pillar of fire appeared before their eyes. It separated into tongues of fire that engulfed each one of them. They were all filled and equipped with the Holy Spirit and were inspired to speak in tongues—empowered by the Spirit to speak in languages they had never learned!

Acts 2:3-4 TPT

My wildfire, my Holy Spirit! He is the mighty one I have promised you. Holy Spirit showed up with a violent blast, a roar of wind, and pillars of fire because they all tarried to birth the church of Jesus Christ. Oh, the unity and oneness of their cry to God. My beloved, my promise is for you too. I will baptize you into Holy Spirit fire, and you shall receive power. You will be completely engulfed in love, new wine, and unleashed power.

And the Spirit will rest on you and equip you for ministry. Your mouth will speak in unknown tongues (languages) called tongues of fire. It comes forth like lightning and sounds like other languages. It is a highly desirable creative language of light. This miracle prayer language is prayed as the perfect will of God every time. The Spirit groans deeply for things we don't even know to pray about. But you can be sure he is heard by God and answered by faith. Let your heart cry out today for him. He will lead you, guide you into more profound truth, and show you things to come.

Jesus, I ardently desire the promise of the Holy Spirit. I am believing you for a baptism of fire now! Fill me with his love and power. I want this miracle prayer language by faith and choose to begin speaking in tongues today.

Acts 2:11

Romans 8:26-27

John 14:15-18

_____

_____

_____

BAPTISM OF FIRE

Engagement

See yourself on the edge of a gorgeous river, and the Lord Jesus is in the water before you, beckoning you to come deeper. You are barely dipping into the water. You see the expression on his face, and he is smiling with such love and desire for you that you step in, up to your ankles and knees, until your feet leave the ground entirely. Lost in this beautiful river of glory, the Lord asks you if you want to go deeper into his passion for you. He wants to baptize you into the promise of the Father, the Holy Spirit. Jesus is willing if you are. You listen as he speaks to you about how they all waited in the upper room to be infused with power— the power of love that will never stop burning.

As you relax in the arms of Jesus with nothing but a yes in your heart and eyes for only him, he immerses you in a baptism of fire and power. And you feel his explosive love course through you, lighting every cell in your body on fire. You know you will die for this ecstatic love and never be the same. See yourself as he raises you, laughing in his power and shouting because he just filled you with the most miraculous healing love. You are so overcome that you break out in an unexplainable prayer language called tongues. And it overwhelms and overcomes you and tumbles out of you in words, songs, and praise. All you want to do is witness to the Lord's goodness. It's the Holy Spirit's language of light. With eyes filled with thankfulness, you become so intoxicated with the Holy Spirit's new wine that you know you will want nothing more than union with God himself. And Jesus looks at you with such love, you know you will never stop burning with desire for him.

SET YOUR GAZE

*Set your gaze on the path before you. With fixed
purpose, looking straight ahead, ignore life's
distractions.*

Proverbs 4:25 TPT

You have doves' eyes of revelation, my beloved. Fix your mind on my fiery beauty, and keep watching me. I have set you apart for myself. As life's journey unfolds, I have something special just for you. So don't look to the right or the left, but come straight ahead. Run with me! Your best days are ahead as you choose my highway of light. Yes, yes, yes, I will lead you into an extraordinary destiny of love. Forget about life's distractions, for they are only temporary, but what is unseen is everlasting.

I am giving you a fresh vision and passion for your calling. Come and sit with me and ask to look into these things. It is the glory of kings to search out a matter. I can ignite your heart with so much hope that you will laugh at the things to come. There may be rough seas, but I am in the boat with you. When I say we are going to the other side, that is where we will go. So be anxious for nothing. Speak to the storms, and they will cease before your faith-filled commands.

Jesus, I am called to gaze upon you as my faithful and true champion. I have found the one I love! I have no more use for life's distractions. I am looking into your mysteries. I choose to go after you with whole-hearted devotion.

Song of Solomon 1:15

Mark 4:35-41

Matthew 6:33

RESTORED TO INNOCENCE

And by the blood of his cross, everything in heaven and earth is brought back to himself—back to its original intent, restored to innocence again!

Colossians 1:20 TPT

Oh, my children, I have forgiven you! Shame no longer has a hold on you. The shedding of my blood has restored everything to me, to the stunning beauty of innocence. There is no more condemnation in Christ Jesus. You have been forgiven of every sin by my blood on the cross. You are righteous! You are magnificently holy, clean, sparkling, and fresh. My sacrifice was entirely honorable and has satisfied fully my Father's requirements for justice. Now, give yourself some grace. Take time and forgive yourself, too. You need to love yourself well.

My beloved, you have a new wineskin now! Old wine will not work for you. You need a new adventure as a true son or daughter of God. Inside your heart, you burn to run forward into your destiny! Angels are waiting with your scroll in hand. Religious doctrine will not do; it's fresh bread daily. My heart beats to your deepest dream— every choice for life. Together, we can transform the whole world! You are fully equipped with my power. Are you with me?

Jesus, thank you that my innocence is restored! I shine gloriously without spot or wrinkle! I gratefully run forward now into my deepest dream and desire. I will change this world into beauty again with you!

Romans 8:1

2 Corinthians 5:17

Luke 24:49

HOPE-FILLED FUTURE

*I know what I'm doing. I have it all planned out –
plans to take care of you, not abandon you, plans to
give you the future you hope for.*

Jeremiah 29:11 MSG

Have you yet to hear? I am the everlasting God. The creator of the ends of the earth. And I desire to partner with you. Wahoo! And you know what? There is nothing impossible for me. I know what I am doing, says the Lord God. And I have a good plan for you, my child—to champion you and help you overcome all the obstacles in life. I knew you before I formed you in your mother's womb. I had a dream and an original design for you and wrapped you around it. There will never be anyone as special as you. I made you fearfully and wonderfully; be grateful and praise me.

Then, I hit it out of the park and gave you the Holy Spirit to be at your side to care for you, and he will never leave you. He is a genius, and he explodes with creative life. So, no matter your circumstances, I plan to give you the fantastic future you hope for. Be fruitful, multiply, take dominion, and believe you can do all things through Christ. I want to astonish you with blessings, so get ready to dream big with me!

Father, thank you that your supernatural plans bring such hope and expectation to my future. I adore that you gave me the Holy Spirit. I refuse to believe in anything but your goodness. You are championing my true calling, and I can do everything through you. I believe in me and so I choose to go for it and dream big!

Isaiah 40:28-31

Psalm 139

Genesis 1:28

ONE SPIRIT WITH THE LORD

*But the one who is united and joined to the Lord is
one spirit with Him.*

1 Corinthians 6:17 AMP

Like a river that flows to the ocean, we are infused, united, and joined in a sea of love and truth. Come and drink the waters of life freely! We are of one spirit, with hearts wrapped around each other. We have become one flesh. Nothing can separate you from my love as the Lord of your life. You are astonishingly beautiful to behold! You are full of my glory, and as you behold me, you will go from glory to glory. Come, abide with me in my love.

You live, move, and have your being within me, sweetheart. I have finished it all and given you myself as a gift of grace. Will you receive me? I am omnipotent, omniscient, and omnipresent. And you are my intimate friend. I have supreme power and absolutely no limitations. Use my inheritance as yours to accomplish your destiny. I give it all to you. I breathed my Spirit breath into you and birthed you into new life. Now, we breathe, think, live, and do everything together! Rejoice because I loved you so much that I gave myself up for you.

Jesus, I love you! We are together now in oneness—face-to-face. I am in you, and you are in me. Our hearts beat together forever. You are my one desire!

Acts 17:26-28

Ephesians 5:30-32

Galatians 2:20

_____

_____

_____

CHANGE IS IN THE AIR

Get up, my dear friend, fair and beautiful lover—
come to me! Look around you: Winter is over;
the winter rains are over, gone! Spring flowers
are in blossom all over. The whole world's a
choir—and singing!

Song of Solomon 2:10-12 MSG

If you listen, the fragrance of the Holy Spirit in this season is whispering: "Change is in the air." Arise, my love! I am calling you near. I am drawing you with my passion to my heart. In my majestic splendor, I will cover you with my wings and show you marvelous things to come. I am moving to do a new thing in the days to come. Keep your heart sanctified and uncompromised. Nothing less than heaven on earth will do.

As I whisper words of encouragement, receive my blessing, favor, and healing. I am calling you! Walk beside me as my beautiful companion, and you will become a fruitful garden overflowing with my goodness for the nations. New life is about to burst forth from your heart! Songs are filling the air with awakening! The world is humming in harmony! I have heard the prayers of my holy people. Acceleration winds are blowing and my bride will arise and shine forth with the new day.

Jesus, yes, I agree that change is in the air! I am excited to have been born for such a time as this. Thank you for giving me courage and covering me under your mighty arms of power. I will go forth as your fruitful garden filled with songs of awakening!

Psalm 91

Isaiah 60:1-2

Song of Solomon 4:16-5:1

HUMBLE YOURSELF

If you bow low in God's awesome presence, he will eventually exalt you as you leave the timing in his hands. Pour out all your worries and stress upon him and leave them there, for he always tenderly cares for you.

1 Peter 5:6-7 TPT

I am the wisest warrior of all time! I say grace, grace to the mountains! I stretched out the north over empty space, and hung the earth on nothing. Relax and trust my love for you. To whom shall you liken me? I am your God and your light! My name is Jehovah Nissi, your Mighty God, fighting with a banner of love to champion your destiny.

Bow low as all valiant warriors do before their royal King. Humility and honor are the essence of nobility. I will lift you up, darling, and exalt you to the highest places of light. Trust in me with all your heart, for I have your best strategy in mind. My dearest, don't try to figure it all out because I am never late. Dance with me, sing with me, and cast all your cares, worries, and weight upon me. Delight yourself in me, and your dreams will become reality.

Jesus, I am a warrior clothed in humility before you. It is my pleasure to submit fully to your extraordinary leadership. I gladly cast every care and anxious thought on you. Yes, you can do anything when I believe you. It's my pleasure to dance with you in the light!

James 4:6

Proverbs 3:5-6

Psalm 55:22

FRAMING UP CREATION

*By faith we understand that the worlds were framed
by the word of God, so that the things which are
seen were not made of things which are visible.*

Hebrews 11:3 NKJV

Oh darling, creation is awesome to behold. The worlds were framed by faith with my friendly letters of light. They are words of truth that strike with lightning power. They are spoken from the purest heart desire, vividly imagined, and directed into a targeted action! And I never pull back my faith. I am a faith God. I will birth it forth, nourishing it with love to completion. The result is a world stunning in fruitfulness with seeds that are self-producing.

Even before one mountain was sculpted, Wisdom was at my side, dancing and rejoicing before me. I set the pillars in place. And when I spoke, my Holy Spirit trembled and vibrated over glorious waters, creating beautiful order out of chaos. Dearest, it's all being held together by love. I am breathing in and through all of it.

You also have a part to play as a priest, king, and prophet to bring order and restoration. I release the power of your breath and tongue to bring forth creative words of power. It is one of my greatest gifts to my children. Let's co-create this world through your faith-filled prayers and decrees. They will build a great foundation of love for all to see.

Oh, Father, thank you that my life is a tiny mirror reflection of yours. I want to create my life with words full of power like you. I want to prophetically release my breath with the Spirit and see my words manifest on the earth. Yes, I delight in your creation, and I adore imitating you.

Proverbs 8:22-36

Genesis 1:2

Proverbs 18:21

DREAM BIG

He stretches out the north over empty space; He hangs the earth on nothing.

Job 26:7 NKJV

I dreamed of a glittering tapestry of trillions of stars that you could enjoy every night. My heavens are vast, miraculous, and strikingly beautiful. They are your playground to explore. When I created the earth and its 5.972 metric tons, I hung it on nothing. My power is unlimited, and I give you, sweet child, my awesome nature.

I topped this by even centering eternity in your very own heart. So vast is your own heart that what you see in the sky pales by comparison. I made you, my beloved, to be able to contain all of me. Therefore, you are valuable beyond measure. You are the very temple of the Holy Spirit. You are indeed fearfully and wonderfully made. The great I AM dwells in you; of whom shall you be afraid?

Be in awe of who I am and who I made you to be. Invite me into your dreams because I want to do for you far above all you can imagine. I speak my dreams into being, and they hold fast. You can speak out your dreams, too.

Ask big! Ardently imagine, vividly desire, and enthusiastically act upon your dreams. All kinds of dreams. What do you have to lose? I am releasing you into limitless possibilities. You have a canvas to paint. Are you ready, my brave artist?

Jesus, you created all the wonders of heaven for us to enjoy with you. Wow! And to top this, you placed your unsearchable and vast eternity in my heart. What an honor. Thank you that I am incredibly valuable. I am going to jump into the big dream of your heart for me. My potential is limitless!

Ecclesiastes 3:11

1 John 4:4

Ephesians 3:20

NOW FAITH

*Now faith is the substance of things hoped for, the
evidence of things not seen.*

Hebrews 11:1 NKJV

Do you desire to bring the dreams of your heart into reality? Well, I have made you a precious covenant. Find the promise in my word; speak it, see it, fight for it. Don't waiver because I want to bless you right now. Today is the day of salvation. Take me at my word. My promises are yes and amen. Pull it in from heaven until you can apprehend it. Your promise has to become so real to you that you possess it now.

The woman who pulled on the hem of my garment had one thing in mind. She was going to get her miracle. That's what you do when you ask me for a promise. Your expectant faith is the substance of your hope until it becomes the evidence of things not seen. It's the challenge of faith. I want you to ask me for it, my child. So use your faith for it now. Prove my will to the world. Don't let your promise stay on the table. There is nothing too hard for me!

Jesus, I am breaking into new levels of faith. I refuse to waiver. I have extraordinary potential to walk in now faith and will prove the good news to the world. I am confident that you will answer my prayers!

Matthew 9:20-22

Matthew 3:2

James 1:6-8

TRANSPARENCY

*At each and every sunrise you will hear my voice as
I prepare my sacrifice of prayer to you.*

*Every morning I lay out the pieces of my life on
the altar and wait for your fire to fall upon my heart.*

Psalm 5:3 TPT

Yes! Lay your heart on the altar, and my fiery love will fall on it. My darling child, I am not a distant God. I want you close, right next to my heart. Like King David in the Psalms, I have promised that you can be vulnerable with me about your life. I know things sometimes go differently than you expected. But I love transparency. We can talk about things intimately and then transform them by my fire through prayer. Expect me to burn up every stumbling block to your breakthrough.

I am passionate about your freedom. I am championing your cause! I am far more in love with you than you know. I have thousands of thoughts about you and your destiny, as many as the grains of sand on the seashore. And I hold them all in a special treasure box for you. I am hoping you will come and sit with me so I can reveal them all to you. I love to teach you and show you the things of the Kingdom. Let's be together; your voice is so sweet to my ears, and your face is lovely.

Father, what a great promise! I will come running to you with my heart. I will share my struggles as we talk and give them to you. Let your fire fall on all the pieces of my heart. I am excited for the breakthrough!

Psalm 139:17-18

Song of Solomon 2:14

Romans 12:1-2

_____

_____

_____

BOOK OF LIFE

Engagement

See yourself in your sacred place. Relax and breathe in deeply the unconditional love of God all around you. The Father comes into view, sees you, and comes running to you and kisses your neck. He picks you up and tosses you in the air with great joy. Feel his love and protective nature over you. He is your treasure. Before he formed you in your mother's womb, he knew you.

He beckons you to follow him to a bench in a beautiful library. It smells like books and wisdom and knowledge in this library. Today, he pulls down an extraordinary book; it's your book of life. He shows it to you excitedly. Deep in the recesses of his heart, he had a dream about you and a unique destiny for your future. Ask him to show you what is in the book. Then, see if you can flip through the pages. Pay attention to anything you discern. He wants to show you he made you for love and goodness and to create beauty on the earth. Ask him what scripture he wrote on your heart when he formed you. Smell the fragrance of heaven all around you. Look into your Father's eyes of love. Thank him because he absolutely adores you.

He asks if you would stand before him as he puts a robe and a ring on your finger and crowns you with royalty. Feel the weight of it. He is commissioning you to represent his Son, Jesus, as an ambassador. Let him show you how. Let him show you your gift and your assignment. And he wants to seal this into your heart now as he pours anointing oil over you, for you were born for such a time as this. Bask in the blessed closeness of your Father. He is everything you need.

FINAL WORDS
FROM THE AUTHOR

I pray that this book has brought you close to the Father's heart and increased your passion for intimacy with him. He looks upon you as the apple of his eye and you are his most valuable treasure. He loves having a truly vibrant relationship with his children, not a religious one. You are chosen, holy, and dearly loved, and you belong to him along with the family of God forever. I bless you with the revelation of your identity. He wants you to know over and over about your royal privileges as his child and the incredible power you carry by believing in him.

Jesus, as his Son, is a fantastic friend, savior, and adventurer. He will lead you into the grandest and most meaningful life ever! I was pulled out of the clutches of chronic illness by giving my life to Jesus at age 50. It was nothing short of a miraculous feat by a Savior who specializes in hard cases. My heart for you is, don't wait another minute. If he did it for me, he can do it for you.

If you want to receive all that Jesus has done for you and make him your Lord and Savior, then say this prayer:

Beautiful Jesus, thank you for loving me and dying on the cross for me. Come into my heart—I believe in you and that you are the Son of God. Forgive all my sins, lead and guide me through life, be my Father, and fill me with joy, peace, and your loving Holy Spirit. Thank you for all the benefits of your redemptive promises and for giving me eternal life. In the name of Jesus, amen.

"*Most assuredly, I say to you, he who hears my word and believes in him who sent me has everlasting life, and shall not come into judgment, but has passed from death into life. John 5:24*"

ACKNOWLEDGMENTS

This work would not have been possible without the support of my husband, Rich, whose generous heart carried me through the many long hours of writing. He steadfastly believes in me and champions me on every level for which I am so grateful. Even when I seemed to be behind doors for hours with the Lord, he encouraged and blessed me to continue. We had long discussions about my writing and considered together how to put it into a framework that would benefit others.

I also want to acknowledge my amazing friend, Debbie Dundas. She has relentlessly prophesied and counseled this devotional into being for many years now. She would prophesy to me: "The Lord has given you his pen to write devotionals." I contended in prayer with those words many times. But I never seemed to have the grace to start, until covid hit in 2020. Then I had the time and I began writing in my prayer studio. I am grateful for her beyond measure and her ability to hear the Lord's wisdom.

ABOUT THE AUTHOR

Nancy Ann Johnson is a licensed minister ordained through the Women in Ministry Network (WIMN) and has trained with Bethel School of Supernatural Ministry. Nancy is passionate about our generation engaging Jesus in the glory. She and her husband attend Bethel Church in Redding, CA. For more information about Nancy, see her website: engagingjesus.com

OTHER RESOURCES BY NANCY

Ask For Your Miracle

"A must-read book full of key foundational truths and testimonies of God's love and promises..." — Evg. Daniel Kolenda

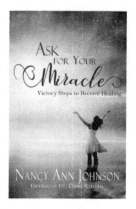

Are you ready to live life to the fullest? This comeback story will thrill your heart to hope and dream again. Jesus was able to save my life and restore me completely. God loves you and is fighting for you to live a life full of victorious breakthrough. There is a very real spiritual battle for your life and you will learn to pursue him until the door for your miracle is open too. Ask for Your Miracle!

https://www.amazon.com/dp/1098769236

Our Covenant of Healing

The world needs hope! And it needs the knowledge of God's healing power! He wants to awaken us to what has been given to us at the cross. When you receive Jesus as your Lord and Savior, you have a right to it. After years of debilitating pain and sickness, Jesus miraculously healed me and got me back on the right road fully restored. In this course you will  learn how to receive and pray for healing with faith. There are four videos and a full workbook including journaling, prayers, activations, Bible study, and decrees.

https://wisdom.xpmedia.com/p/our-covenant-of-healing

Made in the USA
Monee, IL
21 December 2023

50258031R00122